Geographic information systems at work in the community

Zeroing In

Andy Mitchell

ENVIRONMENTAL SYSTEMS RESEARCH INSTITUTE, INC.

PUBLISHED BY
Environmental Systems Research Institute, Inc.
380 New York Street
Redlands, California 92373-8100

The information contained in this document is subject to change without notice.

Opinions expressed in this book are the individual's own, and do not necessarily reflect the opinions of his or her employer.

Environmental Systems Research Institute, Inc.

Zeroing In: Geographic Information Systems at Work in the Community

ISBN 1-879102-50-1

Contents

Preface

The past three decades have seen a quiet revolution in the way people view their neighborhoods, towns, and cities: a revolution brought about by the computer technology known as GIS, or geographic information systems. ESRI has been involved in the GIS field almost since its beginnings. And for more than twenty-five years now, our main goal has been to make GIS technology as widely available as possible so people can use it to solve real problems. With GIS, people are now using computers to analyze all types of issues with geographic data, and their decisions are better-informed than has ever been possible before. The age of the digital map is here.

Although GIS has grown immensely in the last fifteen years, though hundreds of thousands of people now use the technology, and although it affects the daily lives of millions, most people remain unaware of GIS and its impact. Andy Mitchell's book, *Zeroing In,* presents a dozen stories about what people in towns and cities are doing every day with GIS. It shows GIS being used by almost everyone in a community: police officers, business people, planners, property owners, students, and many others. While you read about what GIS means to people and society, you will also be gaining an understanding of how GIS works, and of how you could use it yourself, in your own community.

Today computers are cheaper and faster than ever, GIS software is easier to use, and geographic data is readily available. Whether you work in the public or the private sector, in *Zeroing In* you'll see how you can apply GIS to save time and money in your work. If you're active in your community, you'll gain insight into how GIS can enhance the quality of life for you and your neighbors. If you're a student, you'll be introduced to some of the many professional opportunities opening up in this fast-growing field.

The application of GIS is limited only by the imagination of those who use it. I believe GIS is revolutionizing how we work, and how we solve problems. That's what makes GIS so exciting.

Jack Dangermond
President, ESRI

Acknowledgments

The idea for this book originally grew out of discussions with Clint Brown, Manager of Software Products for ESRI. The approach to the topic was further refined through informal talks with a number of people, most notably ESRI president Jack Dangermond, and ESRI staff members Michael Waltuch, Rich Turner, and Chuck Killpack (who envisioned another book altogether). Through the duration of the project, Clint Brown provided the guidance to make sure the original vision was realized.

The people whose stories are presented in this book made available their time, and patiently explained how, and why, they use GIS. Many others who are not mentioned by name in the book provided valuable background information. Thanks are due all of them. Any omissions or inaccuracies in the book are solely my responsibility. For arranging interviews, and for providing tours, photos, GIS demonstrations, and maps, I am especially grateful to (in order of appearance): Barry Tibbetts, Town of Kennebunk; Felipe Gorostiza, PACDC; Liza Casey, Mayor's Office of Information Services, City of Philadelphia; Tom Pedersen, University of Pennsylvania; Steve Rutkowski, Sears, Roebuck and Co.; Kurt Menking, Bexar Appraisal District; Mark DePenning, City of Greenville; Michael Slagle, Blue Valley School District; Stuart Loosley, Cherokee Metropolitan District; Keith Massie, Metro Regional Services; Todd Kroh, Star Enterprise; Randy Raymond, Cass Technical High School; Andreas Olligschlaeger, Pittsburgh Bureau of Police; and John Hester and Cynthia Albright, Washoe County Department of Community Development.

I also wish to acknowledge all of the organizations who granted permission to include a description of their GIS application and/or a map for one or more of the sidebars in the book. In most cases, the text that appears was excerpted and edited from original text provided by these organizations for *ARC News,* the *ESRI Map Book,* or other ESRI publications.

Several chapters in this book include background information, quotes, or images that were originally collected for other ESRI publications. In particular, additional material for chapters 3 and 9 was provided by Laura Lang via articles that originally appeared in *ARC News*. Some material that appears in chapter 5 was originally compiled by ESRI's Graphics Department for a video entitled *GIS in South Carolina: A Cooperative Venture.* Similarly, chapter 10 includes material that was collected for an ESRI video entitled *GIS in K–12 Education,* and from interviews conducted by *ARC News* staff.

A number of ESRI staff members played key roles in the creation of this book. Michael Karman diligently edited several drafts to weed out excessive technical language and generally make the stories much more readable. Insightful comments on early drafts of the book were provided by Judy Boyd, Laura Feaster, Christian Harder, Betty Martinez, Karen Rossi, and Michael Waltuch. Pamela Townsend created the artwork, while Eric Laycock had the immense task of processing the many photos and other images. Both Gina Davidson and Michael Hyatt (who also did the copyediting and final layout) worked on the design. The necessary legal permissions were obtained by Peter Schreiber and Elsy Anderson, working under a very tight deadline. Finally, Judy Boyd managed the publication of the book.

Many others at ESRI contributed to the research, design, review, or production of the book, and I thank them for their efforts. Thanks also go to Bill Miller, ESRI's Manager of Educational Services, for making staff from his department available to help with final production. Jack Dangermond and Clint Brown provided ongoing support for this project, and I am grateful to them for encouraging me to write this book.

Introduction

In recent years people have been taking more responsibility for running their own communities, from deciding about education and public safety to planning growth and development. But running a community is not easy. Even within the smallest neighborhoods people often have differing points of view. In many towns, less and less money is available for public services. Having good information about the people, places, and things in the community is critical for making decisions that are practical and for working more efficiently.

Since geographic information systems came into common use in the early 1980s, more and more people have used computers to get detailed, up-to-date information about their community in the form of digital maps. But even more people who could be using GIS have yet to discover it. It's not for lack of books on the subject—a number of books about GIS exist. Some explain how GIS works from a conceptual or technical perspective. Others address the management side of GIS—how to implement it in an organization—while many other books teach how to use GIS software. But few books have shown how real people actually use GIS.

This book does just that, introducing what GIS is and how it works by showing some of the many ways people are using GIS to solve everyday problems in their communities. In these "tales from the digital map age," people talk about why, and how, they use GIS. You'll see GIS put to a variety of uses: quickly finding an address in an emergency, creating efficient delivery routes, drawing new school boundaries, comparing the health of children from different neighborhoods, tracking the change in crime throughout a city, and many others.

For many years, GIS was a specialized field, composed of people whose sole job was to build geographic databases, perform analyses, and create maps. And while many still do specialize in GIS, many more use GIS as just one of the tools of their job, like a word processor or an electronic spreadsheet. Some use GIS software and data right out of the box, adding in their own data. Others customize the software with menus and buttons designed specifically for their data and their tasks. Still others combine GIS with information from other programs, such as spreadsheets or computer models. In this book, you'll see all of these approaches in action. And you'll see examples of how these systems look on screen, as well as maps that have been created and printed out on paper.

The book presents other information besides the stories of what people are using GIS to accomplish. To get an idea of how GIS works, you can read the full-page sidebar in each chapter that presents the computer "story-behind-the-story." Other sidebars throughout the book take a look at the most common types of GIS data used in towns and cities. While each chapter stands on its own, the GIS concepts presented progress from basic to more advanced. So if you're reading the technical details, the earlier chapters present information that might be helpful to know in the later chapters.

What all this information presents is how GIS affects the daily lives of all of us, those who use it as well as those who benefit from it. You may even start to think about how GIS can play a role in your work and your community.

Zeroing In

Geographic information systems
at work in the community

Dispatchers

in Kennebunk,

Maine, use GIS

to help speed

police, firefighters,

and ambulance

crews to the scene

of an emergency.

1 Emergency Dispatch

"It must've happened a month and a half ago, maybe going on two. It was before Memorial Day—I know that." Paul Bennett, who works in his dad's café in Kennebunk, Maine, is recalling an accident that happened right outside the café. "Pete and his girlfriend were sitting back here," he says, motioning toward the windows. "It happened real quick. She jumped up and yelled, 'Oh my God, someone got hit by a car!' I immediately got on the phone."

Bennett talked to Kathy Baker, communications supervisor at the emergency dispatch center. "I remember she asked, 'Who's calling, where is it, and what's the situation?' That's it. Three questions." Baker remembers dispatching the police and ambulance crew to the scene. She had no problem giving them the location of the accident—everyone in Kennebunk knows where Bennett's café is. "They were here quick. I'd say within five minutes," says Bennett, who knew the bicyclist who'd been hit. "They brought him to the hospital. No broken bones. He just got scraped up a little bit. He was pretty fortunate."

Not every emergency is as easy to pinpoint as the one in front of Bennett's café. Baker remembers another incident, this time from a frantic caller in rural west Kennebunk. "They could not tell me which road they were on—they were off a dirt road; it was a long driveway," she recalls. Baker has handled many such calls in her eighteen years with the police department. "When a person is upset, it's very hard to extract information from them," she explains. Even getting their correct address or the color of their house can be difficult. And people tend to misjudge distance when giving directions. "Sometimes, what they perceive as a mile is way off. So you can't really depend on somebody telling you it's a mile down on the right-hand side," says Baker.

Kennebunk has a year-round population of 10,000. But the number of residents—and emergency calls—swells during the summer when tourists flock to the area's scenic coastline.

Dispatcher Suzy Cabral activates the emergency dispatch system.

From a town hall office two floors above the dispatch center, Barry Tibbetts serves as Kennebunk's tax assessor and also as the town's GIS coordinator. In the latter role, it's his job to see how GIS can be used to help the different departments operate more efficiently. After meeting with Tibbetts in late 1995, it was obvious to Baker and the other dispatchers that GIS could help them quickly find a caller's location. The emergency dispatch systems some big cities were using were way too expensive for a small town like Kennebunk, so town officials contacted a private consulting firm, Planet One Software, to see if they could develop a GIS-based dispatch system that would run on a small desktop computer.

The developers at Planet One worked closely with Kennebunk's dispatchers to find out what would help them the most. The system they developed, called E-911 Dispatcher, uses the caller's phone number to look up the address and display a map showing where the caller is located. Baker and the other dispatchers can also use the system to create a map of the shortest route from the police or fire station to the location of the emergency.

The system proved its worth shortly after it was first installed in May of 1996. Dispatcher Suzy Cabral, who works the swing shift, was on duty. An elderly woman from west Kennebunk called for an ambulance. She was home alone and having severe abdominal pain. When Cabral asked for her address, the woman replied that she was on Middle Road. Cabral knew it wouldn't be easy for the ambulance to find her—the houses in that part of town are far apart and set way back from the street.

Cabral activated E-911 Dispatcher, and a street map of Kennebunk appeared on the computer screen. She clicked a button and the system immediately displayed the woman's phone number, name, and address. Cabral could see the woman was actually calling from an address on Old Alfred Road, rather than Middle Road. In her distress, the woman had become confused. Cabral confirmed the woman's name and clicked another button to zero in on her location, which the system had

The system uses the phone number to look up and display the caller's address.

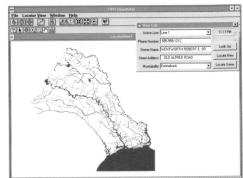

shaded bright red. Within twenty seconds of picking up the phone, Cabral had found the woman's correct address and had a map of the location up on the screen.

At that point, Cabral got on the radio and announced the call over the police and fire channels. Officer Andy Belisle picked up the call and headed out toward Old Alfred Road. With Cabral's help, Belisle quickly found the woman's house. Meanwhile, Cabral clicked a couple more buttons and E-911 Dispatcher created another map showing the shortest route from the central fire station (where the ambulance is dispatched from) to the woman's house. Cabral radioed the directions to the crew that was en route. The ambulance soon arrived and took the woman to the hospital.

In situations like that, before they had the dispatch system, the dispatchers and emergency response personnel had to rely mainly on their own knowledge of the area to locate the caller. Sometimes they would resort to skimming over paper maps, trying to pinpoint the location based on whatever information the caller could provide. Now they can quickly create a detailed map of the location using the caller's phone number, name, or address. The system also lets dispatchers display the locations of fire hydrants, storm drains, power poles, and other information that might be important in an emergency.

Most of the information came from the town's existing database, which town officials and staff found they couldn't use as it was. "We

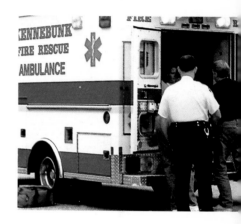

Cabral clicks a button to zero in on the location. The system shades the caller's lot red and displays surrounding lot lines, building locations, and streets.

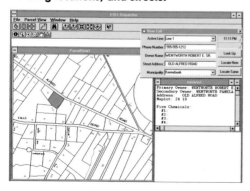

Cabral clicks another button to display the shortest path from the police or fire station to the scene of the emergency.

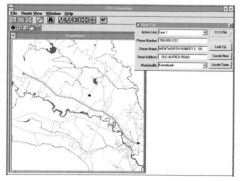

"When a person is upset, it's very hard to extract information from them. Knowing where that call is coming from—seeing it on the screen—it's tremendous."

KATHY BAKER, COMMUNICATIONS SUPERVISOR

had to go back and clean up all our data," says Tibbetts. To do that, they used a combination of aerial photography from a private firm and digital street data from the U.S. Geological Survey. They also had students from the University of Southern Maine drive all the streets and map them using a GPS unit to get accurate locations for streets and intersections.

Town staff also had to add every resident's phone number to the system. For now, public safety staff have to keep the phone numbers updated when people move. But when Maine's Enhanced-911 system comes on line, Kennebunk's dispatch system will get the caller's street address directly from that system. The telephone company will maintain the link between the phone numbers and the street addresses in a central database. That way, the information will always be up-to-date.

While an outside contractor did most of the GIS database development, the Town of Kennebunk also received several grants from state and federal governments to hire students to do some of the work, including digitizing building footprints and scanning photos of all the buildings in town. That information is also in the system, so, if necessary, dispatchers can give emergency response teams a description of the caller's house.

GPS

GPS, or Global Positioning System, is a network of satellites that send signals to earth-bound receiving units. The signals can be used to get the latitude and longitude of any point on earth. The most accurate receiving units can calculate their position within a meter of their actual location. GPS has many uses—from helping aircraft and ships navigate to locating lost hikers. It has also become one of the main sources of data that can be used in a GIS. A car or truck with a receiving unit mounted in it drives the streets of a town to record the locations of streets and intersections. The locations of other features, such as telephone poles, manholes, and fire hydrants, can also be obtained using GPS.

You can use GIS to quickly find and map the location of a person, building, or event. That lets you see who or what is closest to the location and how best to get there. Emergency dispatchers in Kennebunk, Maine, use a GIS-based dispatch system to find the location of people calling for help so they can give exact directions to emergency crews.

What the system does...

1 Gets information about the location. The dispatch system is tied into the police department's phone line. When an emergency call comes in, the dispatch system automatically gets the caller's phone number.

555-4201

5 Winding Brook Drive	**555-8642**
90 Old Alfred Road	**555-4201**
24 Sea Garden Circle	**555-3121**
26 Sea Garden Circle	**555-1734**

2 Searches the GIS database for a match. The dispatch system uses the phone number to find the parcel that matches.

3 Displays the location. Once the system finds the matching parcel, it draws the parcel in the center of the screen and shades it red. It also draws other features from the database, such as streets and building outlines. The dispatchers know exactly where the caller is located and can direct emergency crews to the scene.

More examples of using GIS to find a location...

◆ Voters in Ontario, California, can call the local library on election day to find out where their polling place is. The caller gives his or her nearest cross street, and a clerk uses the GIS to display a map of the location, find out which precinct the caller is in, and provide the location of the polling place, with directions, if necessary.

◆ VISA cardholders can use the World Wide Web to find a nearby ATM that takes VISA. The cardholder enters a street address or intersection, city, and state. In a few seconds, the GIS displays a map showing the cardholder's location and the three nearest ATMs. The cardholder can then zoom in to get a more detailed map.

An alternate way of finding a location...

A GIS can also use a street address to find a location. It first locates the right street using the street name, the street type (e.g., "Road" or "Avenue"), and prefix (e.g., "East" or "West"). Then it uses the house number to find the correct block (234 State Street is in the 200 block). The GIS knows in which direction the house numbers increase, so it can calculate where the address is along the block (234 State Street would be about one-third of the way from the beginning of the block). Finally, since the GIS knows which side of the street the odd and even numbers are on, it offsets the address to the correct side, and draws its location with a dot or other symbol.

200 Block of State Street

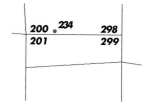

Dispatching the closest ambulance in Montreal, Quebec

The Urgences-santé Corporation provides ambulance service to the Montreal metropolitan area. The company uses GIS to decide which ambulance to dispatch to an emergency. Each ambulance carries a device that sends its current coordinates to the dispatch center. When a call comes in, the dispatcher gets the coordinates for the five ambulances stationed around the city. The GIS calculates how long it would take for each ambulance to get to the scene. Once it finds the closest ambulance, the GIS displays the fastest route for that ambulance, taking into account traffic, road construction, and current weather conditions.

The "Wedding Cake House" is a popular tourist destination. In an emergency, dispatchers can simply enter the name of the landmark into the dispatch system to display the maps and other information.

At the request of the dispatchers, developers at Planet One are also adding locations of local landmarks, parks, and other public areas to the system. "Sometimes people will call up and say 'I'm down in front of the Wedding Cake House,'" explains Baker, referring to a well-known landmark. "Well, that's not an address, but you still want to be able to zoom to those points of interest." Once that information is in the system, dispatchers will simply need to enter the name of the landmark to pull up the maps and other information.

The dispatchers aren't the only ones in town using GIS. The tax assessor, town clerk, and planning department also use GIS to help track growth and development. Town Manager Richard Erb's goal in setting up the GIS was to have a single system that all the departments could use. Erb and other town officials have worked hard to make sure the departments share the information that goes into the GIS database.

Creating fire dispatch zones in Tacoma, Washington

The City of Tacoma Fire Department used GIS to create response zones for its stations. The GIS determined the closest fire station to each street by calculating the travel time from each station outward along the streets. The resulting map provides accurate response zones, so firefighters from the closest station will be sent to the fire. The map also shows which stations are next closest, and so can be called for backup.

That information is now also available to the public, via the town's World Wide Web site. Erb says the GIS has helped establish better cooperation between the town's departments and helped make them more efficient. "We've had to rethink a lot of the way things have been done," notes Erb. And that, he says, has helped the town save money while providing better service to its residents.

The residents of Kennebunk may not be aware of the role E-911 Dispatcher plays in getting police, firefighters, and ambulance crews to the scene faster. But Baker and the other dispatchers know how vital it can be when they need help locating a caller. "Knowing where that call is coming from—seeing it on the screen—it's tremendous," says Baker.

Nonprofit community development corporations in

Philadelphia use GIS to help plan housing projects in

depressed neighborhoods, and get funding for them.

2 Housing

On a Friday afternoon under overcast skies, El Bloque del Oro is alive. This stretch of Fifth Street, running through the Fairhill neighborhood, is the heart of Philadelphia's Hispanic community. Lined with colorful banners, the street vibrates to the pulse of Latin music blaring from radios. Cars double-park while shoppers hurry in and out of stores.

Away from Fifth Street, though, another picture of the neighborhood emerges. In one block, the sole building is an abandoned, six-story factory, its windows broken out, its walls covered with graffiti. On another block stands a line of abandoned row houses without windows, doors, or plumbing, inhabited by squatters and rats. An empty, trash-strewn playground, the swings missing and the asphalt cracked, occupies a nearby street corner.

Once the industrial center of Philadelphia, Fairhill began its decline as factories and workers moved to the suburbs after World War II. Today, 64 percent of residents live below the poverty level. Less than 40 percent own their homes, and the rental housing is overcrowded. Many residents live in houses or apartments with high rents, in some cases without running water or even electricity.

But there are signs of change. On one corner a lush green lawn dotted with young trees surrounds new apartments for the elderly. A few blocks away is a spotless street lined with fully repaired and repainted row houses. Nearby, more new apartments are under construction. These and other projects in the neighborhood are all due to the efforts of HACE, the Hispanic Association of Contractors and Enterprises.

With its offices right on Fifth Street, HACE is offering hope to the residents of its community. HACE is one of about 75 nonprofit Community Development Corporations, or

The Fifth Street shopping district in north Philadelphia's Fairhill neighborhood is the center of the city's Hispanic community.

CDCs, in Philadelphia that are trying to revitalize the depressed neighborhoods of the city. Since 1990, HACE has not only developed over 150 units of housing in Fairhill and neighboring St. Hugh, but has also helped bring new businesses to the Fifth Street shopping district.

HACE and the other CDCs get some project financing by applying for grants from the City of Philadelphia Office of Housing and Community Development. Most of that money comes from the federal Community Development Block Grant program. But with a $1.5-million cap on any specific project, the CDCs must also line up other sources of funding.

Getting even one project funded and built is a major effort. And all the residents want their block to be the one to get a project. The result has been individual projects scattered throughout a neighborhood. "You see a development here, a development there, but not a comprehensive impact," says Steve Culbertson, director of the Philadelphia Association of Community Development Corporations. In the early 1990s, both the city and a number of the CDCs began to realize they needed a more coordinated approach to redevelopment. According to Culbertson, many CDCs had already developed informal plans. "We wanted to flesh those out—bring in the

research and bring in the maps," he says, "and make them work."

To test the approach, the office of housing provided funding for about a dozen neighborhood groups, including HACE, to create five-year plans for their communities. One goal of the plans was to show each neighborhood's need, and potential, for redevelopment. With support from the housing office, HACE and several of the other groups used GIS to create maps showing the conditions in their neighborhoods.

To develop their plan, HACE worked with the Community Development Institute, a

Fairhill was once Philadelphia's industrial center. Factories were left vacant when companies moved to the suburbs in the 1950s and '60s.

Most properties in Fairhill are valued at less than $5,000.

Market Value ($)
1 - 999
1,000 - 1,999
2,000 - 4,999
5,000 - 9,999
over 10,000

nonprofit group that offers planning assistance to neighborhood organizations. With information provided by the city, the consultants created a series of maps showing the current conditions in Fairhill. The map of market value begins to tell the story. Almost all the properties in the area are valued at less than $5,000 (dark green on the map), many of them less than $2,000 (light green). And even many of the commercial properties along Fifth Street are valued less than $10,000 (pink). The problem, explains Felipe Gorostiza, programs coordinator for the CDC association, is that with such low market values, property owners don't think it worthwhile to fix the places up. Absentee landlords often just let their buildings go and stop paying property taxes.

Another map confirms that tax delinquent parcels are widespread throughout Fairhill. The amount owed in back taxes ranges from $100 (light blue) to over $5,000 (purple). Says Gorostiza, "There are whole pockets where there's no financial incentive for owners to do anything with these properties—the market value is less than what is owed in back taxes." Many of these parcels have been abandoned and are vacant.

Because market values are so low, many of the old row houses in the neighborhood have been abandoned by their owners.

The shaded properties are tax delinquent. For many properties, the value is less than the amount owed in taxes.

Fairhill has a high percentage of publicly owned and absentee-owned properties.

HACE has rehabilitated older row houses and resold them to low-income families, as well as building new rental units and housing for the elderly.

A third map shows that the number of publicly owned (red) and absentee-owned (blue) properties is extremely high. These properties are generally less likely to be well maintained than are owner-occupied houses. Many of these are also vacant.

Taken together, the maps clearly show the dire condition of the housing market in the neighborhood. Gorostiza sums it up: "When you start putting these things together you start to realize what you're up against in trying to rehabilitate any part of this area. People may still decide to do it but it certainly lets you know it's a long haul."

The GIS-generated maps have proved to be an integral part of HACE's, and the other neighborhood groups', five-year plans. Says Culbertson, "We needed to go to the city, to foundations and corporations, to get the funds to make a difference. The plans have helped us to do that. We have the vehicle and we have the research to back it up."

The key people who helped the neighborhood groups get started using GIS were Liza Casey, currently GIS program director for the Mayor's Office of Information Services, and Tom Pederson, a consultant working for the city's office of housing. They began by collecting data from various city agencies. Parcel boundaries and information on assessed value came from the Board of Revision and Taxes. Information on tax delinquency came from the Revenue Department and the information on vacancy from the Department of Licenses and Inspections. Casey and Pederson used the GIS to merge this data with the parcel boundaries so it could be mapped. Then each CDC received the data for its neighborhood.

geographic coordinates

You can locate any place on the surface of the earth by measuring its relative distance north or south and east or west of a known point. These north-south/east-west measurements are the geographic coordinates of that place. The GIS stores the locations of features by storing their geographic coordinates. Latitude/Longitude is a common way of specifying geographic coordinates.

You can use GIS to create up-to-date customized maps of a neighborhood, town, or city; maps that can focus attention on a specific issue by presenting information about the place in a graphic way. Several community development corporations in Philadelphia used GIS to map the status of housing and commercial property in their neighborhoods, helping generate investment in new projects.

What they did...

1 Decided what the maps should show. The neighborhood groups wanted to show the need for investment in the neighborhood overall, as well as to identify blocks that might have the most potential for redevelopment (e.g., blocks with many vacant properties).

2 Assembled the data in the GIS. With help from staff at the City of Philadelphia, the groups obtained the GIS database of property boundaries for their neighborhood. The properties were already linked to the parcel tax database. They also linked the parcels to other computer databases of tax delinquent and vacant properties.

APN	Mkt. Val.	Delinq.	Absentee
1813-058	$4475	$110	N
1813-080	$2380	$0	N
1813-139	$11310	$455	Y

3 Created the maps. Since the GIS tags each property with all its characteristics,

it was easy for the groups to create the set of maps. For one map, they color-coded the properties based on market value; for another, by amount of tax delinquency; and so on. The maps were included in each neighborhood's five-year plan.

How the GIS makes a map...

To draw a map using GIS, you tell the GIS which features to display. The GIS stores the "geographic coordinates" of all the features. If you're mapping individual locations, such as customer addresses, the GIS draws a symbol at the spot defined by the pair of geographic coordinates for each address. For linear features, such as streets, the GIS draws lines to connect the points (coordinate pairs) that define the shape of each street. For areas, such as a parcel of land, the GIS can draw its outline or fill it in with a color or pattern. You specify the symbols, lines, and colors to use, or you can let the GIS pick them for you.

312 Forsyth

A coordinate pair defines an address

Coordinates define the shape of the street

The GIS also stores the characteristics of each feature. So for each street the GIS may store a name, the number of lanes, posted speed, and pavement type. You can use these characteristics to specify how to draw the features. You could draw four-lane streets with a thick line and two-lane streets with a thin one. The GIS automatically draws each street using the right type of line since it knows which streets are four lanes and which are two.

Name	Lanes	MPH	Paving
15th ST	2	35	Asphalt
14th ST	2	35	Asphalt
Peachtree	4	45	Asphalt

"These are very dramatic presentation tools. People can see the map, see their neighborhood; and this bright color shows them just what's going on here. It really wakes people up."

FELIPE GOROSTIZA, PACDC PROGRAMS COORDINATOR

HACE and the other groups had a lot of this information before using the GIS, but it was mainly available as statistics, such as the total number of vacant properties or the total amount owed in back taxes. Having this information in the GIS allows the groups to actually show the locations of these properties and see the patterns within the neighborhood. That helps them decide where they should invest their limited redevelopment dollars. Notes Gorostiza, "These are very dramatic presentation tools. People can see the map, see their neighborhood; and this bright color shows

them just what's going on here. It really wakes people up."

Casey and Pederson are now working with the CDCs to develop standards for their maps so, for example, all the groups would use the same five classes of tax delinquency and the same colors to represent them. That way it will be easier to compare the situation between various neighborhoods. Casey also hopes to expand the use of GIS so that more of the CDCs get the computer hardware, software, data, and training they need to create maps for their five-year plans.

Besides the work with the CDCs, Casey is also helping other departments at the City of Philadelphia use GIS. The Water Department is currently using GIS to analyze storm water overflow. The Public Works Department is putting the locations of all 200,000 light poles into the GIS to track maintenance of street lights. And to comply with the Americans with Disabilities Act, the city uses GIS to make sure there are wheelchair curb cuts near bus stops, stores, and other services. Much of the data

Finding industrial redevelopment sites in Birmingham, Alabama

The City of Birmingham's Office of Economic Development uses GIS to help developers find potential sites for industrial redevelopment. The GIS produces maps of the sites along with data about each, including total acreage, zoning, assessed value, and distance to utilities, interstate highways, and airports. The information helps developers compare and evaluate potential sites. "The unique graphical capabilities of our GIS application allow developers to envision viable sites where only potential now exists," says John Gemmill, OED's head of administrative services.

needed by the various departments overlaps. For example, almost all the departments use street and parcel data. Casey helps the departments share that data. "The degree of cooperation between our departments is really nice to see," she says.

GIS is helping city workers do their jobs more efficiently and create a better quality of life for all the city's residents. It will also continue to help the CDCs as they strive to improve their neighborhoods. Concludes Culbertson, "The CDCs are actually very good at making a difference in their community and building hope. That's really a lot of what it takes to make a change."

classes

Classes represent groups of features that are similar to each other, for example, land parcels of similar value or census tracts with roughly the same number of school-aged children. Classes show the conditions or patterns in a place, rather than exact information about individual features. When you work with a GIS, you tell it how many classes to make, what the range of each class should be, and what color or pattern to use to draw each class. The map legend tells readers what each class represents. The way you set up the classes—the number of them, and the range of values for each—can result in very different maps, even though the underlying information (e.g., the value of each parcel) hasn't changed.

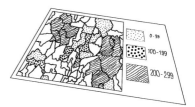

Neighborhood redevelopment in Louisville, Kentucky

The Louisville Development Authority used GIS to map historic architecture in the Smoketown neighborhood. The authority recognized that the historic buildings were an asset that could bring new development to the neighborhood. The information on the location and status of the buildings was obtained through field work and in-house research, and given to the Louisville Public Works Department to create the maps.

Customer service reps at the Sears distribution center

in Ontario, California, use GIS to create routes for

home delivery of appliances and furniture.

3   **Home Delivery**

It's a hot, hazy August evening in San Bernardino. Couples and families with small children cross the sea of asphalt that surrounds Inland Center Mall, heading for the air-conditioned comfort of Sears. In the appliance department this Monday night, shoppers mill about, checking price tags and opening refrigerator doors. One young couple finally decides on a Kenmore, and the lanky salesman who's helped them types their address and phone number into the computer. Then, to their question, he assures them with a smile that their new refrigerator will be delivered between 8 and 12 Wednesday morning.

By 3:30 the next day, Marshall Tappe, a customer service rep, is racing the clock. He has less than an hour to finish scheduling the deliveries for the more than 300 customers who are expecting their refrigerators, dishwashers, couches, and other items some time Wednesday. At the Sears distribution center in Ontario,

California, about 12 miles from the Inland Center Mall, Tappe peers into an oversized computer screen while speaking rapidly into his telephone headset. "Hi, ma'am. My name is Marshall. I'm calling from Sears Delivery. And I just want to verify an address for delivery of a refrigerator for tomorrow..."

By 4:30, the truck drivers have the next day's delivery routes in hand, the forklift operators are picking merchandise off the giant warehouse racks, and the other customer service reps have begun their evening round of phone calls, letting the customers know when to expect their new furniture and appliances.

"At Sears we define home delivery as getting the right merchandise to the right customer at the right time," says Steve Rutkowski, a senior systems manager for Sears. That may sound simple and straightforward. But unlike bus routes, which have fixed stops and regular schedules, home

Sears' Inland Center Mall store in San Bernardino, California, is just one of several served by the Ontario distribution facility.

Sears prides itself on being the "best of the best" in home delivery. Customer satisfaction means repeat business.

company, to develop a GIS-based system that would create more efficient delivery routes. The system they developed finds the location of each customer and assigns the customer's delivery to a truck. Then, for each truck, it figures out the best order to make the deliveries in and the best route along the streets between the stops.

In November 1995, the new system was installed at the Ontario distribution center. Tappe now uses it to create the daily routes for half a dozen distribution centers located in Southern California, Las Vegas, and Yuma, Arizona—all from his desk.

Today is an average Tuesday—just over 300 deliveries to process. First, the routing

delivery routes have to be created from scratch every single day. A lot of factors are involved—how large the merchandise is and how heavy, how much the trucks can carry, where the customers live, how long it takes to get from one house to the next, and how long it takes to unload and install each appliance. Plus, the truck has to arrive within the promised four-hour delivery time.

In the early 1990s, Sears was delivering within the promised time window about four out of five times. The company wanted to improve that record and maybe even reduce the window from four hours to two. "Our goal," says Rutkowski, "is for customers to meet us during their lunch breaks and not spend the entire day waiting for a home delivery." So in 1994, Rutkowski and other managers at Sears began working with ESRI, a GIS software

system automatically assigns each address a location on the street map stored in the GIS. It takes about twenty-five minutes.

The system locates all but fifteen of the addresses. Tappe has to figure out why those customers weren't located, and make sure they get added to the map. Usually an incorrect address was entered at the store or the house is on a new street that isn't in the GIS yet. Tappe checks the first address. He clicks on the street displayed on the screen to list the address ranges. All the addresses on that street are five digits long, but the house number on the customer's order is only four. A digit must have been left off when the address was entered into the computer at the store. Tappe makes a quick phone call to the customer to get the correct address. He changes the house number on the order and clicks a button on the screen. The system places a small purple dot on the street map. "OK, it's matched. Wonderful!" he exclaims, and moves on.

The next address is on a street that isn't in the system. So Tappe types in the names of the nearest major cross streets, which he gets from the customer's order. A small red x appears on the map. Tappe has the system zoom in and display the intersection. Positioning the cursor over the intersection, he clicks the mouse to enter the location—it's close enough to make

sure the customer will be on the right delivery route. The next day, the driver can call for exact directions.

Tappe works fast, spending only a few minutes on each address before moving on to the next. At 3:00, any orders that have come in during the last hour have to be processed. Finally, all the addresses have been successfully located. It's now 3:40.

At this point, the system starts doing its work. First it groups the delivery stops, based on how close they are to each other. The goal is to assign at least sixteen stops to each truck.

Tappe first makes sure every customer's address has been located on the map.

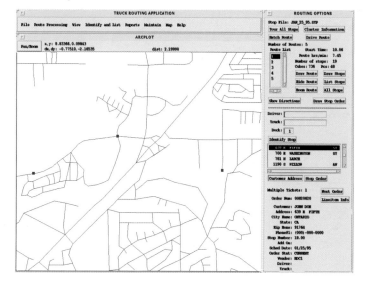

It checks to make sure the total merchandise on each route doesn't exceed the capacity of the truck in either volume or weight, shifting stops between trucks if necessary. Next, it figures out the best order for the stops on each route, based on the delivery time window—morning, afternoon, or evening—and the amount of time needed for the driver to unload and install the appliances or furniture at each stop. Finally, the system calculates the fastest path between the stops, in the order they've been assigned.

When the system has finished, Tappe displays the routes on the screen. He checks to make sure they're as circular as possible, so the drivers don't have to backtrack or travel too far out of their way. If necessary, he can manually re-sequence stops, or reassign them to another route. But all that takes more time and can push the routing process dangerously close to the deadline. Today, all the routes look good. At 4:15, Tappe faxes the route reports to the various distribution centers. And the warehouse managers, forklift operators, and truck drivers take over from there. Tomorrow, Tappe will be back in front of the computer to go through the whole routine again.

Before they had the GIS, workers created the routes by hand. They would place a large sheet

The system groups stops that are close to each other into routes. (The colors and symbols indicate different routes, and morning, afternoon, or evening delivery.) It then sequences the stops for each route and finds the best path between them.

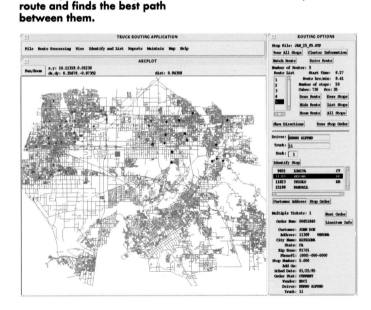

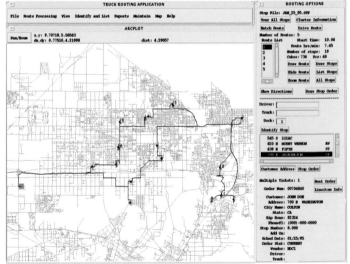

You can use GIS to find the shortest path between two points. That can help you get to your destination fast or help you create efficient delivery and pick-up routes. Customer service reps at Sears use a GIS-based system to map the best routes for their home delivery trucks.

What the system does...

1 Locates the stops. The GIS uses the street address to place each customer on the map.

2 Groups the stops. The system then assigns each stop to a route according to the number of available trucks, the size and weight of the merchandise, and how close the stops are to each other.

3 Sequences the stops. The system determines the best order to make the stops, based on the time the delivery was promised. It avoids making the truck backtrack or travel too far out of its way.

4 Finds the shortest path. Finally, the system finds the shortest path between the stops for each route and prints a list of directions for the driver.

How the GIS finds the shortest path...

The GIS checks the distance from the starting point, or origin, to the next intersection in each direction. It picks the intersection closest to the origin and continues from there. That way, it identifies the intersections most likely to end up in the final shortest route. As it goes, it builds a list of the intersections it has reached and the distance from the origin to each, repeating the process until it reaches the destination intersection. It then draws the shortest path between the stops using the list of intersections.

Using time instead of distance...

In many cases, the best route is better measured in travel time than in mileage. A GIS can calculate a fastest path by substituting time for distance. Some systems use the speed limit and the length of the street to calculate a travel time for each block. Others use average travel times calculated from traffic data, often with different values based on the time of day the trip occurs.

More examples of using GIS to find the best path...

◆ In Ontario, California, residents who are elderly or disabled can call a Dial-A-Ride service staffed by volunteer drivers. The dispatcher uses GIS to calculate the shortest path between the caller and the driver, and then gives exact directions to the driver.

◆ To quickly restore electrical power after a storm, Boston Edison often runs a new cable to bypass the interrupted cable. Workers use GIS to find the best path for the new cable through available conduits. The GIS considers the size of the cable, which manholes are flooded, and other factors.

Delivering bottled water in Southern California

The Sparkletts Water Company of Los Angeles uses GIS to help create more efficient routes to deliver bottled water to its customers. The routes are based on customer sales territories. "The GIS determines which route to place customers on and instantly matches them to their new route sales representatives. The old process used to take as much as three days," says project leader Steve Essayan. As customers are added or removed from a given territory, the GIS can adjust the routes to balance the load between drivers.

of glass over a street map of the area. Using grease pencils, they'd locate each address and put a dot on the glass. Then they'd create the routes, working back and forth between the customer orders, the size and number of available trucks, and the location of each stop. If they needed to re-sequence a stop, or assign it to another route, they'd erase the lines on the map and redraw them. Depending on the number of deliveries, it usually took two or three people with extensive knowledge of the area several hours to create the routes just for one warehouse. Now it takes Tappe just over

an hour to do the routes for all seven distribution centers in the region.

The key to the process is having a good database of streets. Sears purchased the street data from a company that maintains and sells the information for the entire country in a format the GIS can use. Tappe or the other customer service reps can digitize new streets directly into the GIS from subdivision maps or other sources. In addition to the actual map of the streets, the information in the database includes the speed limit and the length of each street. This information is used to calculate a travel time for each block, which is in turn used to create the fastest route between the stops.

Right now, the system prints out a list of directions for each truck, which Tappe faxes to each warehouse along with the route reports. The drivers use the directions for reference, in case they get lost, instead of "stopping at gas stations and making a lot of phone calls," notes Rutkowski. Soon, the system will also

digitizing

Digitizing is a common way to take the information on a paper map and put it into a GIS. You place the map on a special table—called a digitizing tablet—that has a fine wire mesh beneath the surface. As you trace over the features on the map using an electronic puck, the geographic coordinates of the features are stored in the computer.

address matching

Address matching is a way of getting a list of street addresses into a GIS so you can see where they are on a map. The GIS matches a street name and number from the list to the same street name and range of address numbers on the map. It figures out where along the street the specific address is, based on the address ranges of the block. It then assigns geographic coordinates to the address so it can be displayed on the map as a point. The key to successful address matching is making sure the addresses on the list are correct and as specific as possible. For example, if the list has "349 Orange" but the map has a North Orange St. and a South Orange St., the GIS won't know where to put the address. Then you have to find out the correct address, change it on the list, and have the GIS try again.

Students and school locations in Garden Grove, California

What's in an address database? An address database consists of a set of people, events, or things that have a known street address. Each address has at least a street name and number. It often also includes the street type (Rd, Blvd) and a directional prefix or suffix (East, NW). Each address also has a location in geographic coordinates. That way it can be drawn on a map. Any amount of information may be associated with an address—details about the people living there, the business or building at that address, or an event that occurred there.

Where does address data come from? In most cases, the address information is already in a computer database: student records, customer records, an organization's members, and so on. Usually, these addresses need geographic coordinates assigned to them. The GIS will automatically do this using a process called "address matching." In some cases, the address is supplied "on-the-fly," as when someone calls 911 and gives their address to the operator.

What can a GIS address database be used for? Just about anything for which you need to know the location of a street address:

- Locating customers and seeing where they are in relation to your stores
- Locating students to create attendance areas and bus routes
- Mapping the locations of crimes and looking for patterns and trends
- Responding to emergencies

How is address information made available? Many private companies and organizations sell databases of information that include a street address. In some cases, the addresses are already geographically located so they can be mapped in a GIS right away. You can also use your own list of addresses by address matching it to a digital street map in the GIS.

"Since employing this GIS-based system we've been able to hit about 95 percent of our deliveries on time. It's really made a difference."

STEVE RUTKOWSKI, SENIOR SYSTEMS ANALYST

be able to create a map for each stop to help guide the drivers even more.

Besides reducing the amount of time needed to do the routing, the system creates more efficient routes, helping Sears improve its delivery service. "Since employing this GIS-based system, we've been able to hit about 95 percent of our deliveries on time—within a two-hour time window," says Rutkowski. "It's really made a difference." He quickly adds, "We're not out there advertising two-hour delivery yet, but we're proving it can be done."

The home delivery system is being installed in Sears distribution centers across the country. Meanwhile, Rutkowski is starting to look at other uses of GIS, such as routing service technicians to customers' homes. He's found that by using GIS to create the routes, Sears can decrease the amount of time technicians spend in transit and the amount of overtime they have to work. Sears is even beginning to use GIS in the warehouses to route forklifts. It's similar to routing home delivery trucks, only instead of customers' houses, the stops

Sears uses GIS to find the best routes for forklifts as they pick merchandise from the warehouse racks and carry it to the loading dock.

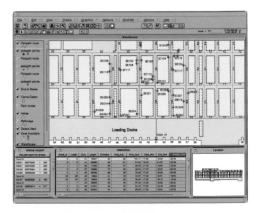

are the different racks where the merchandise is stored. And instead of routing trucks along streets, the GIS routes forklifts along the aisles in the warehouse. Using GIS increases the number of orders a forklift operator can fill in an hour. That means customers will get their appliances and furniture sooner.

Providing better service to its customers is what prompted Sears to start using GIS. The company prides itself on being "the best of the best" in home delivery, according to Rutkowski. GIS is helping Sears maintain that reputation.

Tracking shuttle vans at Dallas/Fort Worth Airport

Park, Ride and Fly of Irving, Texas, uses GIS and GPS to track the exact location of its shuttle vans as they travel between airport hotels, terminals, parking lots, and home base. A GPS receiver in each van continuously radios its current location to a GIS at home base, which displays that location on a map as the van travels its routes. "The system allows me to know exactly where my vehicles are at all times," says operations manager Tom Kennedy. "The result is quicker response times, better service, and greater coverage without adding vehicles."

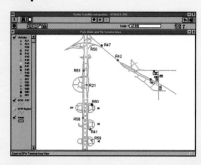

Property owners in Bexar County, Texas, use GIS on public computer terminals to find out if their property has been assessed fairly.

4 Fair Taxation

Downtown San Antonio. Late April. Under the giant Tower of the Americas in Hemisfair Park, Fiesta is in full swing. But inside the offices of the Bexar Appraisal District a few blocks away, the mood is less festive. In the public research room, a young couple stands at the desk of customer service rep Nancy Gonzales. The woman grasps the notice she and her husband have just received, valuing their house $6,000 higher than last year. This means their property taxes will go up another $175. The woman says she knows the taxes are needed for schools, police, and roads; she just wants to make sure they're not paying more than their fair share.

Gonzales explains that they first need to find out the values of the other houses in their neighborhood. A pained look crosses the man's face as he mutters that they shouldn't have to spend all day looking through files and reports. But Gonzales is already pointing to the computer terminals in the corner, where other people are looking at maps and printing them out. With one of those computers, she says, they can get all the information they need in just a few minutes.

Scenes like this one have not been uncommon in San Antonio in the past few years. Several corporations moved their headquarters to the area in the early 1990s, creating a big need for housing. With demand outstripping supply, home prices went up, along with property values and taxes. Over the long term, an increase in property value is generally good news for an owner. But the sting of higher property taxes is immediate.

Appraisers for the Bexar Appraisal District, which includes San Antonio, assess properties by looking at such characteristics as the size of the house and lot, the age of the house, and its type of construction. They also look at recent sales of similar homes nearby. All this information is entered into a computer model that calculates the current value of each property in a neighborhood. That appraisal appears on the notice received by property owners every April. And under Texas property law, owners have the right to protest a valuation they think is unfair.

In 1993, the district decided to create a computer system that would allow property owners to quickly find the information that led to their valuation. Having access to the same information the appraisers used would give owners a better idea of whether to file a protest. The district wanted a system that would present the information in a way that was easy to see and understand. So district staff used GIS to develop the Customer Query System,

which lets homeowners create maps that compare their property to surrounding ones.

The couple sit down at a terminal and type in the account number of their parcel. The map that appears shows the outline of their lot and several adjacent lots, along with the dimensions of all the lot lines. Their lot is in the center, marked with a star. The map also lists their account number, their names, and their street address.

They select the "Total Value" option from the menu on the screen, and they see on a new map that their property is valued at $91,800, just as the notice said. The house to their right is valued slightly higher, but the one on the left is much lower, $83,000. Three other parcels on their street also have lower values. All

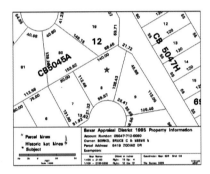

Property owners use the Customer Query System to get a map of their lot with its dimensions (above). They can compare the value, living area, and value per square foot of their property with their neighbors' properties. They can also display a map of the houses that have sold in the past year, along with the sales price of each.

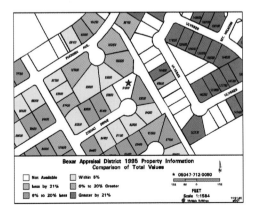

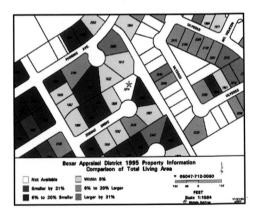

of these parcels are colored green. According to the map legend, that means the parcels are valued up to 20 percent less than theirs. They remember that the house next door has only two bedrooms to their three; maybe the other green parcels have smaller houses as well.

To check their suspicions, they display the map showing total living area. They were right; the parcels that were green on the map of total value are green on this one, too. They realize what they really need to see is the map showing total value per square foot. On that map all the properties on their street are colored yellow, that is, all valued about the same on a dollar-per-square-foot basis. Their appraised value looks like it's not out of line after all.

They still can't believe, though, that their house is worth over $91,000. So they display the map of current sales information. The house next door to theirs, which is the same age and only 50 square feet bigger, sold for almost $10,000 more than theirs was valued at. The couple stops by Gonzales' desk on the way out, only fifteen minutes after they had sat down. Holding a set of printed maps, they tell Gonzales that they need to give it some more thought before filing a protest.

Before the Customer Query System was in place, property owners couldn't get this kind of information until halfway through the appeal process, which could be several weeks after filing the protest. District staff had to compile the information from various sources,

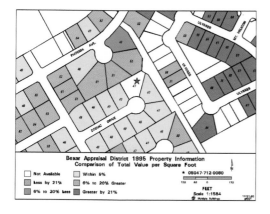

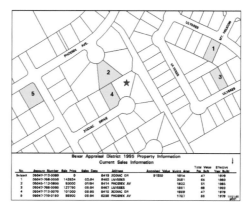

"There are times when we have people three or four deep trying to get to those terminals."

KURT MENKING, GIS MANAGER

Appraiser Joe Hudson notes that the system "can more than accommodate any question that might arise in a protest situation."

Some in the district offices were wary of the system at first. As Kurt Menking, the district's GIS manager, recalls, "That product initially upset a lot of [our] people, because we created this product to let customers see all this information." But district staff soon dropped their objections when they saw how it helped streamline the appeal process.

The system has also become very popular with the public. Come appraisal time, the local newspapers always run articles that mention it. "When those articles come out we have a lot of people come down. There are times in that room when we have people three or four deep, trying to get to those terminals," says Menking.

which could take up to forty hours of staff time per protest. With the system in place, the information is available to homeowners up front. Gonzales, who is now a rural appraiser with the district, says, "It's real quick. It'll show if they are undervalued, overvalued, or within the range of everybody else in their neighborhood. They can spot it right away."

If a property owner does decide to file a protest, the case may end up in a hearing before the Appraisal Review Board. The query system is used here as well. Chief Residential

Getting parcel information over the Internet in Oakland, California

Oakland residents can find out about their property on the World Wide Web. In the "map room" of the Community and Economic Development Agency, they use GIS to enter a street address or assessor's parcel number and display a map of their property and the surrounding area. They can zero in on a parcel and display an aerial photograph in the background or zoom out to show the full city. A future version of the system will let people find and display all the parcels that have certain characteristics, such as a particular value or lot size.

You can use GIS to find out what features are near a location and get information about them. This can save a lot of time and effort, especially if you need to look at many locations on a daily basis. Property owners in San Antonio, Texas, use a GIS at the Bexar Appraisal District to compare surrounding properties to theirs, so they can decide whether to file an appeal on their assessment.

What the system does...

1 Finds the location. To identify their parcel, property owners enter either their street address or the account number from their assessment notice.

2 Defines the box around the location. The GIS centers the map on the parcel and calculates a box—or "geographic extent"—around the parcel.

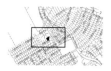

3 Selects the features within the box. Out of the 400,000 parcels in the district, the GIS selects just those that fall within the geographic extent.

4 Gets information about the features and displays it. The GIS compares each selected property to the owner's property for each characteristic (e.g., value, size) and creates color-coded maps. Owners can see right away whether their property has been valued the same as comparable ones.

Other ways of finding what's nearby...

If you need to find out what's within a certain distance of a location, you can create an area, or "buffer," around the location. You tell the GIS which property or other feature to create the buffer around, and specify the distance. The GIS creates the buffer and selects all the features that lie within it.

Properties within 300 feet of a zoning variance, Glendale, California

The GIS also knows which features share boundaries. That lets you get information, for example, about just those properties bordering selected parcels of land.

Adjacent parcels

Another example of using GIS to find what's nearby...

The City of Bellevue, Washington, uses GIS to find out which properties will be affected by street improvement projects. They create a 300-foot buffer around intersection projects, and a 100-foot buffer around roadway projects, and overlay the buffers on top of a parcel map. They then know exactly which property owners to notify before construction starts.

When a homeowner asks for a specific map—for instance, one showing assessed value—the system compares the value of each parcel in the mapped area to the value of the owner's parcel. It then calculates the difference between the two as a percentage and shades each parcel on the map accordingly. Using the same color scheme on each map ensures that maps are consistent among properties across the county. Any of the more than 300,000 residential parcels in the county can be used as the target property to create a set of maps.

Hudson and his appraisers are continually collecting information about both existing and new properties—over 100 different characteristics in all, from a variety of sources: deeds, building permits, and field inspections, among others. This data is constantly added to the system, so the maps always reflect the latest information.

COGO

COGO or "coordinate geometry" is one way to enter lot lines or other surveyed data into a GIS. You enter the distances and angles of the lines using the computer keyboard, and the GIS figures out the geographic coordinates. The information can also be transferred directly into the GIS from electronic survey equipment that stores the data as digital files. Using COGO is an alternative to digitizing an existing paper map.

For years, the district has been using a computer database to store the parcel information. Having the GIS allows the district to link all the information to the parcel boundaries and display it graphically. When it got the GIS, the district obtained parcel boundaries for the City of San Antonio from the city's Engineering Department. For areas outside the city, the district contracted with a private firm to digitize the boundaries from aerial photographs.

With the system in place, the main job now is keeping up with the rapid growth of the region and making sure new parcels are accounted for. The GIS has made this ongoing task much more efficient. As Lydia Sauceda, supervisor in the GIS Department, explains, "Whereas before, I would actually draft it in manually, with a scale and a mechanical pencil, now I do it with a [digitizer] puck and COGO."

Having all the information available as maps has made the system useful to the appraisers as well as the public. Residential appraisers use the GIS to help create neighborhood boundaries by analyzing the age, construction type, and size of houses, and by grouping like properties. Agricultural appraisers use the GIS to calculate acreage for the large parcels they have to assess. "They're using a lot more map information than they ever used before. It's just part of their everyday jobs," notes GIS Manager Menking. All the parcel information in the GIS

aerial photograph

Taken from a small plane at a low altitude (around 1,000 feet), aerial photographs cover an area of about a half-mile square.

Usually a series of photos is taken to cover an entire community. Once scanned into the computer, the photos can be registered to geographic coordinates and displayed with other features in the GIS. They are often used to create or update information on parcel boundaries, streets, and land use.

What's in a parcel database? A city or county parcel database contains the parcel boundaries (lot lines) that denote land ownership. The database also includes the characteristics of each parcel, often over a hundred different pieces of information about each.

Aerial photo with digitized lot lines

Where does parcel data come from? The boundary information is digitized or scanned from paper maps, drafted and digitized from aerial photos, or entered on the computer keyboard using COGO. The parcel characteristics come from deeds, building permits, field inspections, and other sources.

Land use around proposed mall, Albuquerque, New Mexico

What are parcel databases used for? Almost anything having to do with land ownership. Here are some examples:

◆ Property tax assessment

◆ Land use and zoning maps and studies

◆ Economic development analysis

◆ Real estate transactions

How is parcel information made available? Many local governments have set up public-access terminals that let you see the information and create custom maps. Others will create custom maps for you, for a fee. Some cities and counties also sell their parcel database on tape or CD–ROM at a nominal cost.

is available from the district on tape for about $100. While most people won't need all this information, a number of private companies have purchased the data for research and consulting.

The main benefit of the GIS, from the public's point of view, continues to be the Customer Query System. It has given property owners access to the information they need about their property. It has made the appraisal process easier for both the public and the appraisers. And it has helped ensure that all properties within the Bexar Appraisal District are assessed fairly.

Public access to property information in Lincoln County, North Carolina

Lincoln County residents can get information about their property using a public computer terminal in the tax assessor's office. The 8½-by-11-inch sheets they print out contain maps of their lot and neighborhood, a photo of their house, and ownership information. The page also lists which voting and school districts the property is in, and whether it's in a flood zone. The information all comes out of the county's GIS. "The greatest benefit in having the information has been in making it available to virtually anyone," says Jay Heavner, Lincoln County's tax administrator. "They can come in and look at what we have, free of charge, which has been a real hit with taxpayers and county officials alike."

The Greenville, South Carolina,

Fire Department uses GIS to help

evacuate residents during an

emergency.

5 Evacuation

11:08 A.M.—A call comes in to the desk of Assistant Fire Chief Tom McDowell. Two trucks have collided near a residential neighborhood. One driver is dazed and bleeding; the other is unconscious and pinned inside his truck. Witnesses report that a gas is leaking from containers on one of the trucks. McDowell, who is also the fire department's emergency management coordinator, immediately dispatches a hazardous materials response team to the scene, and calls in police to close off a four-block area around the site.

11:27 A.M.—Wearing protective suits, masks, and oxygen tanks, the response team arrives on the scene. While some team members attend to the crash victims, others begin trying to identify the chemical producing the gas. If it's toxic, the neighborhood may need to be evacuated.

11:53 P.M.—McDowell meets up with police officials a few blocks from the accident site. They need to know what the gas is so they can decide if an evacuation is called for. Time is critical—any hospitals, nursing homes, or schools in the area will need advance warning to get everyone out ahead of the gas. On the other hand, an unnecessary evacuation will be costly and disruptive.

12:06 P.M.—The report from the hazardous materials team crackles over the radio: It's deadly chlorine gas. The area needs to be evacuated immediately. McDowell and the rest of the emergency management team start estimating where, and how far, the toxic plume will spread. After checking current weather conditions and their hazardous materials guidelines, they draw on their maps an area a quarter-mile wide, extending a mile downwind of the accident.

12:11 P.M.—Police officers are notified to start evacuating residents from the area.

Greenville, South Carolina, is the largest city in the northeast corner of the state and a major textile manufacturing center. The fire department has to be ready for all types of emergencies.

In the late 1980s the Greenville fire department staged a mock disaster to find out how well their emergency procedures worked. The results of the drill convinced the city to use GIS to help manage evacuations.

This emergency drill, staged by the Greenville, South Carolina, Fire Department in the late 1980s, led the city to develop a GIS-based evacuation procedure to cope with real emergencies. Greenville, with a population just over 58,000, is the largest city in the northeast corner of the state and a leading textile manufacturing center. The fire department and other agencies need to be prepared to deal with a variety of emergencies, from flooding to an overturned truck carrying toxic chemicals. An emergency response plan put in place some years before had never been tested. So in 1989, fire officials, along with police, the Division of Social Services (DSS), and the Red Cross held the emergency drill to find out how the plan would work in an actual emergency.

In the debriefing following the drill, they realized there were some serious problems. The maps the emergency response teams were using did not have all the street names and address ranges inside the evacuation area. Without this information, it was hard for police to keep track of the evacuation as it progressed. Nor was there a way to locate critical care facilities needing special attention, such as hospitals or nursing homes. And there was an even more serious problem in moving evacuees to predesignated staging areas. As Chief McDowell recalls, "The directions we gave them carried them right through the

plume, simply because we didn't understand where the evacuation staging area was in relation to that plume, and what was the best way for them to get there." The DSS and Red Cross also had no information on how many people were likely to be evacuated, so they could not plan their staffing needs. Nor did they know how much temporary shelter space they would need.

After the debriefing, McDowell met with Mark DePenning, the city's GIS manager, to see how they could develop a GIS-based system that would provide the missing information and do it fast enough to be used in the event of an actual evacuation. "We were dealing with the police, we were dealing with DSS, and we were dealing with the Red Cross," McDowell explains. "So we had a multiagency problem, each one of those having a different need. And there was nowhere we could go to

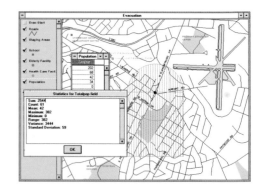

get that [information]. It did not exist at that time. So we used the GIS and created it."

Here's how a typical scenario might unfold using the GIS-based evacuation procedure. When McDowell gets word of a chemical spill, he enters information about the chemical and the current weather conditions into a program on his computer at headquarters. The program calculates how far from the spill the toxic plume is likely to spread, as well as the downwind corridor it will eventually cover. This becomes the evacuation area. In the GIS, McDowell then displays a map of the streets around the accident site and, using the mouse, draws the boundary of the evacuation area. The system checks to see if there are any health care facilities or schools within the area or nearby. In a few seconds, the GIS highlights these on the map and displays a list showing the name of each, along with the address and

"We were dealing with the police, we were dealing with the DSS, we were dealing with the Red Cross ... each one having a different need."

TOM McDOWELL, ASSISTANT FIRE CHIEF

the number of beds or rooms. McDowell quickly prints the map and list and hands them to the evacuation teams.

Next, he has the system sum the number of people who live inside the evacuation area, with subtotals by age group. He radios this information to the police, the DSS, and the Red Cross so they know the scale of the evacuation. Then McDowell maps safe routes to the staging areas. Finally, he prints a complete list of streets and addresses within the area. He hands the maps and lists to the officers heading to the scene. Within a few minutes, all the teams

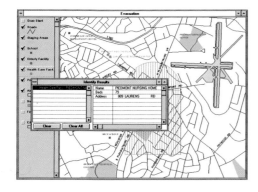
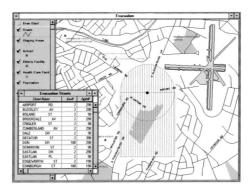

McDowell draws the evacuation area in the GIS and quickly gets the information the evacuation teams need: the names and addresses of schools and health care facilities; the total population within the affected area; and a list of streets.

Police use the list of streets and addresses within the evacuation area to notify residents block-by-block, offering special assistance where needed.

involved have the information they need to carry out the evacuation quickly and safely. As officers finish notifying the residents on each block, they call in to the central command post, which tracks the progress of the evacuation.

Before the city created the GIS-based approach, emergency personnel planned and managed an evacuation using paper maps. They estimated how the plume would disperse based on U.S. Department of Transportation (DOT) guidelines, and drew the area by hand on the maps. "You could say 'OK, the DOT guide says you need to evacuate downwind 1 mile. Let's make it 1.1 miles just to be safe. Let's make it a half mile wide,'" explains Chief McDowell. This was a rough estimate at best, since local weather conditions, terrain, and other factors were not fully taken into account. And it was not very efficient. "You've got all

these different people trying to figure this out on paper maps, and you've got different [map] scales," adds GIS Manager DePenning. Other information, such as the location of hospitals and nursing homes, and the number of people inside the affected area, was hard to get or simply not available.

Now when a toxic leak occurs, McDowell enters information about the type, quantity, and rate of release of the toxic gas, the wind direction and speed, current weather conditions, and other factors into a computer model. The model calculates how the plume will disperse and displays the boundary on top of a street map. Using the streets for reference, McDowell redraws the boundary in the GIS. The GIS then uses this boundary to select and display the information about what's inside the evacuation area.

Siting new fire stations in Rochester, Minnesota

The City of Rochester used GIS to help assess the need for new fire stations. A committee developed scenarios showing which part of the city could be reached within one, two, or three minutes from each possible location. "We had to … look at the city geographically and determine response times according to roads, speed, and congestion. We felt that using the GIS system would be the most appropriate way to do that," says Ron Livingston, division supervisor for the Planning Department. Maps and reports were created for the city council members, who decided to build one new station and to look into possibly relocating two others.

You can use GIS to get information about the people and things in a specific area. The Greenville, South Carolina, Fire Department uses GIS in case of a toxic gas leak or other emergency to find out which streets, schools, and hospitals need to be evacuated. The GIS also calculates the total number of residents within the area, so the Red Cross knows how many shelters are needed.

What they do...

1 Define the affected area. The fire chief uses a computer model to estimate how far the toxic plume is likely to spread, and in which direction. That becomes the evacuation area.

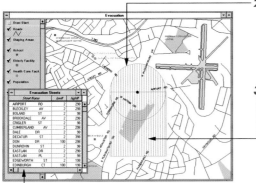

2 Draw the boundary in the GIS. The chief draws the boundary of the evacuation area on the computer screen, using streets as a backdrop for reference.

3 Query the GIS database. The GIS uses the boundary to find the streets, schools, and hospitals that fall within it. It also overlays the boundary with census tracts to find the tracts inside the evacuation area.

4 Display the map and information. The GIS displays a map with the selected streets, schools, and hospitals highlighted. It also lists the address ranges for each street, and the name and address of each school or hospital. The GIS totals the population within the census tracts to find the number of residents affected. The chief relays the information to police and to the Red Cross so they can begin the evacuation.

Other ways of defining the area...

There are several ways to create an area in the GIS, besides drawing it freehand. You could use an existing area, such as a ZIP Code, census tract, or school attendance area. Or you could specify all the area within a certain distance of a place. Whichever method you use, once you define the area, the GIS can list individual features with their characteristics, find just those features that meet some criteria you specify, or create summary statistics for the area.

More examples of using GIS to find what's inside an area...

◆ The Illinois Department of Nuclear Safety used GIS to find residential lots within a contaminated area in West Chicago, Illinois. The department mapped the area using GPS, then overlaid the boundary with the map of lot lines. The information helped them decide where to start and to track the progress of the cleanup.

◆ GIS helped determine who would be affected by noise from the Munich Airport II near the city of Freising, Germany. Different air traffic patterns were mapped and overlaid with population data. The information helped airport planners make traffic patterns that would affect the fewest people.

The first version of the evacuation system did not include the computer model. Fire officials calculated the plume manually, using the U.S. DOT guidelines as before, and then drew it in the GIS. Even so, that system was still a big step forward. "It was really a pretty simple system," says DePenning. "It just was able to provide information that, even though it didn't seem like a lot, was essential to managing the incident." The current version models the plume much more accurately, making it less likely that residents will be evacuated unnecessarily. Eventually, the city plans to improve the system even further by having the GIS take the plume boundary directly from the model. Then Chief McDowell will no longer have to draw the boundary by hand.

The evacuation procedure uses information that was already in the city's GIS. The streets had been drafted from tax parcel maps and then digitized by technicians. The locations of nursing homes, health care facilities, and staging areas all came from the parcel maps as well. Finally, population data, already in digital form, was obtained from the U.S. Bureau of the Census. Now the focus is on maintaining the system. As DePenning notes, "The real issue we've got here is keeping data up to date and having it reasonably accurate."

A toxic gas leak is just one situation the system can handle. If the toxic substance is a liquid, the system can be used to map which storm drains and sewers it might flow into, so emergency personnel can seal and contain the spill. The fire department also uses the system to model worst-case scenarios in the case of an explosion at an industrial site. And a few years ago the system was used to select the least hazardous route through the city when a load of munitions had to be moved to a disposal site.

Chief McDowell hopes he never has to use the evacuation system in a real emergency. But the system stands ready if there is an accident. And while most residents of Greenville may not realize it, McDowell knows the city is much safer than it was just a few years ago.

Responding to earthquake damage in Los Angeles, California

Following the Northridge earthquake in January 1994, the County of Los Angeles Urban Research Section used GIS to create a series of maps for the county's Emergency Operations Center. "The most immediate need was a detailed map of the freeway closures," says systems analyst Laura Armstrong. The department also created a map showing the locations of American Red Cross shelters in relation to damaged areas and closed roads. Another map displayed the locations of all disaster relief applicants along with locations of the temporary Disaster Application Centers to show where more centers were needed.

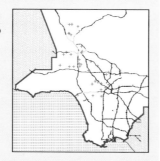

The Planning and Facilities Committee of the

Blue Valley School District in Overland Park,

Kansas, uses GIS to decide where to draw

school attendance boundaries.

6 Schools

The clock shows 7:35. Dave Hill, the school district's director of planning and facilities, looks around the room and tries to call the meeting to order. "I'd like to have you look at the agenda topics for this evening. We have several pieces of information that we'd like to review tonight before we get into the discussion…"

But it's too late. The discussion is already underway. "My concern is we're talking about a border from 213th Street all the way up to 163d—are kids going to be pulled out of their neighborhoods?" asks one committee member. "One of our goals has been to not split subdivisions," agrees another. "Well," points out a third, "the boundary could be drawn in several different ways. It could cut across, or down."

It's another Tuesday night meeting of the Blue Valley School Board's Planning and Facilities Committee. Fourteen members have shown up this chilly December evening to discuss a new middle school that will open in 1997. The school will handle kids from new subdivisions being built in the southern portion of the school district. It will also relieve the overcrowding at Harmony Middle School. The question is where to draw the boundary between Harmony and the new school to the south.

The committee's goal is to make sure both schools have roughly the same number of students. But it's not that simple. Redrawing the boundary means some kids will have to change schools, leaving friends and familiar surroundings. It's not a prospect the kids or the parents relish, and about thirty parents are here tonight to make sure the committee members know it.

Still, the boundary has to go somewhere. As they discuss alternatives, committee

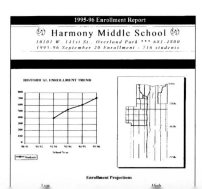

members and parents view a 6-by-8-foot screen hanging from the ceiling. On it is projected a map of the southern portion of the district. One of the committee members ventures a suggestion: draw the boundary along 165th Street. As the woman gives her reasons, Michael Slagle, the planning manager for the school district, clicks a few buttons on a computer sitting on a nearby table. A minute later, the map projected on the big screen changes to reflect the proposed boundary. Then a list of the number of students that would attend each middle school appears alongside the map. The attendance numbers look reasonable. But several parents quickly point out that their kids would have a very long ride to the new school. Another committee member proposes moving the boundary a few blocks south, and Slagle again redraws the map.

Committee members will draw and redraw the middle school boundary map many times before they present their final plan to the school board. And the next month they'll do it all over again for the high schools.

The Blue Valley School District includes most of the City of Overland Park, Kansas, along with parts of nearby Leawood and Olathe, and part of unincorporated Johnson County. It's the fastest growing suburb in Kansas City and among the top thirty fastest growing communities in the United States. Every year, 700 to 1,000 new students move into the district. To handle all these kids, the district has opened fourteen new schools since 1985.

It's up to the Planning and Facilities Committee to redraw attendance boundaries when a new school is built. Committee members try to keep all the students from a single neighborhood together and minimize the distance kids will have to travel, all while trying to make sure none of the schools has too many students, or too few. And with schools opening so rapidly, the committee members want to make sure borders remain in place as long as possible. In a few rare cases, kids have changed schools three times before the fifth grade. Committee member Debby Heasley, whose four children attend Blue Valley schools, says, "That's something this committee takes very seriously and that we try to foresee and prevent."

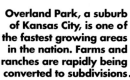

Overland Park, a suburb of Kansas City, is one of the fastest growing areas in the nation. Farms and ranches are rapidly being converted to subdivisions.

Blue Valley School District has built fourteen new schools since 1985 to keep up with the growing student population. Over 700 new students are added to the district each year.

It quickly becomes a complex task. With the rapid growth in the district, the committee needed to find a way to streamline the process while looking at a variety of options. So in 1993, Planning Manager Slagle used GIS to develop a system the committee members could use right in their public meetings.

The system proved its worth the following year when a new elementary school opened. The school had to be built quickly after the City of Overland Park changed the planned use for a 160-acre parcel from commercial development to housing. The nearest school, Cottonwood Point Elementary, had been built to handle no more than 700 students and was already near capacity. With the new houses, enrollment could be expected to jump to almost 900 students. So the district built Heartland Elementary on a 12-acre parcel they bought from the developer. The committee members then had to create a boundary for the new school, making sure they included enough Cottonwood Point students to prevent overcrowding there.

Some of the brand-new subdivisions would clearly be within Heartland's boundary. But the committee faced a tough decision in one neighborhood. The kids all played together and went to school together, at Cottonwood Point. But, to make the numbers of students roughly equal between the two schools, it looked like the kids in the eastern half of the neighborhood would be attending Heartland.

The committee members used the GIS-based system to explore alternatives to splitting the neighborhood. First, they discussed keeping the neighborhood together and putting it within Heartland's boundary. But just by looking at the map they could see that meant some kids within a quarter mile of Cottonwood Point would have to travel a mile and a half to get to Heartland Elementary. So they dropped that option.

They then had Slagle redraw the map, keeping the entire neighborhood within Cottonwood Point's boundary. But when the numbers came up on the screen, they could

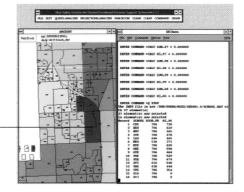

The committee used GIS to decide where to draw the boundary around Heartland Elementary. With this attendance area (shown in blue), some students would have too far to travel to the new school, located in the upper right corner of the area.

With this option Heartland would have too few students to open and neighboring Cottonwood Point (gray area) would be over capacity.

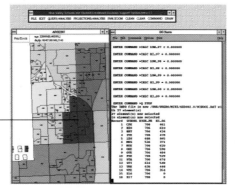

The final decision prevented overcrowding at Cottonwood Point but ended up splitting a neighborhood.

see that under that option Heartland would have only 165 students, not enough to make it worth opening the school. And Cottonwood Point would still be about thirty students over capacity.

Finally, the committee members faced the inevitable. They had Slagle select the eastern half of the neighborhood and assign it to Heartland. The numbers worked—Cottonwood Point dropped to 461 students for the next year, while Heartland would have 434.

The parents in the audience had also seen the options displayed on the big screen. While disappointed that the neighborhood had to be split, they could see that it really made the most sense. Says Slagle, "We showed them that if we went too far over to the east or to the west, viable attendance areas for the new school could not be created." Perhaps most importantly, the boundary change wouldn't be a surprise to the parents when the school board announced it the following January.

Before the system was in place, it took the committee much longer to reach a decision. Committee members would meet to discuss the alternatives, then ask the district staff to have the new boundary maps and numbers ready for the next meeting. The staff, recalls Slagle, would "recalculate everything, write it down on paper, type it up, and bring it back

You can use GIS to draw boundaries in different ways so you can create an area that best meets your needs. Members of the planning committee for the Blue Valley School District in Overland Park, Kansas, use GIS to create attendance boundaries for new schools.

Here's what they do...

1 Set the criteria. Each attendance area has to have a certain number of students so the school will be neither overcrowded nor underused. The area has to be small enough so students won't have too far to travel to school, and should avoid splitting neighborhoods.

2 Combine areas to create the boundary. Committee members select which subdivisions they want to include within the new boundary, and the GIS tags them with the school's code. The GIS knows the number of elementary students within each subdivision, so it can total the number of students within the proposed boundary.

Subdivision	Students
100231	62
100344	51
100267	32
101233	46
101465	16
102298	21
102399	27
102429	12
102688	41
105744	24
105322	43
105245	17
TOTAL	**392**

3 Evaluate the options. Committee members can change the boundary by changing which subdivisions they select. The GIS automatically retotals the number of students. Committee members and parents can focus on the options that have the right number of students to see which would best meet the other criteria.

4 Create the final map. The GIS shades all the tagged subdivisions in one color so committee members can easily see the area they've created. Then they send the proposed boundary to the school board for final approval.

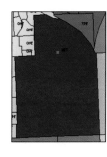

Other ways of creating boundaries...

You can also use GIS to create a boundary by defining an area within a set distance of a location. This is especially useful for locations that have to be at or near the center of the area, such as fire stations. The GIS works outward from the location, totaling the distance along each street until the specified limit is reached. Or, instead of distance, you could have the GIS total up the travel time or the number of people living along each street until it reaches some limit.

You can also create a boundary just by drawing it on the screen wherever you want. Usually you display other information to guide you. If you're creating a sales territory, for example, you'd probably display streets and the locations of your customers.

Another example of using GIS to create boundaries...

The Texas Attorney General's Office uses GIS to analyze legislative districts, both current and proposed. Maps created with the GIS are often used as courtroom exhibits, to show that districts comply with the Voting Rights Act and to examine voting patterns. The office also makes maps available to the public and has assisted interested parties in the creation of legislative and judicial districts as well as city council, county commissioner, and justice of the peace precincts.

the following week." This process would be repeated week after week. Now, since new maps and enrollment figures can be displayed during the meetings, committee members can look at more options in less time.

The system also calculates the average distance students have to travel to each school, by grade level, and estimates how long it will be before a school boundary will have to be redrawn. That helps the committee members decide if the boundaries they've come up with are acceptable, or if they need to go back to the maps.

The system relies on a combination of software programs. Slagle uses a spreadsheet package to forecast enrollment. Then, he explains, "We import that data back into the geographic information system and start doing

Student enrollment is forecast with a spreadsheet package. The numbers are input into the GIS to help create the boundaries.

boundary manipulations to come up with what we hope will be the best plan available."

The enrollment projections rely on a wide variety of data. Slagle gets information on building permits from the City of Overland Park and other cities within the district, and from Johnson County. These agencies also provide information on any changes to the development plan and zoning map. From the district's enrollment records, Slagle knows how many students to expect per housing unit from the various types of housing. He gets information on the number of pre-Kindergartners in each subdivision by analyzing population data and from surveys conducted by the local PTAs. Slagle

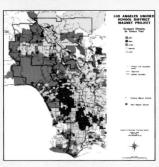

Providing equal access to education in Los Angeles, California

The Los Angeles Unified School District uses GIS to look at where magnet schools are in relation to the ethnic makeup of the district. That ensures that services are provided fairly across the district. The study is part of a larger effort to look at school bus transportation as it relates to the district's student integration program. Using GIS reduces costs and lets the district quickly get accurate answers to questions from parents, community groups, and the media.

"This is one of those tools where [parents] can participate right at the beginning. They can actually see the numbers being generated."

MIKE SLAGLE, PLANNING MANAGER

puts all this data into a computer model he built using the spreadsheet. What he gets back is the projected number of students in each grade for each subdivision, over the next five years.

The GIS uses the subdivision number to link enrollment projections to subdivision boundaries. Slagle created the subdivision boundaries from the county's parcel database, which was already stored in a digital GIS format. When Slagle uses the system to assign a subdivision to a school boundary area, the GIS tags the subdivision as belonging to that school. It then gets the projected attendance for the school by totaling the students in the tagged subdivisions. The GIS does all of this in a matter of seconds.

Creating school boundaries is only one use of the GIS at the district. Once the boundaries are approved, Slagle uses the system to find out who pays for busing. The system uses the shortest routes along the streets to find the houses within 2 miles of each school. Parents

of students in those homes have to pay for busing; beyond that range the state picks up the tab.

Slagle is currently improving the system so school planners can use it to find parcels to build new schools on. The GIS will combine information on each vacant parcel—its size, whether it's in a floodplain, how close it is to a major road, and so on—to find just those sites that meet all the criteria for building a new school. "The end product would be a list of parcel addresses, owners, and appraised value of the property," says Slagle.

In its present role of creating boundaries, according to Slagle, the GIS has improved

Evaluating school bus service in Bellevue, Washington

The Bellevue School District used GIS to help decide whether to continue providing bus service for high school students or have them ride public buses. Since they found that most students who lived more than a mile from school also lived within ¼ mile of a public bus route, the school district decided to issue the students passes for public transportation.

How does a GIS store boundary data?

The GIS stores the boundary lines that enclose a district or other area, identifying it by a unique number and usually also by a name. The GIS also stores information about each area, such as its size, the number of people living within it, and other characteristics.

Where does boundary data come from? Some boundaries are part of a nationwide system (census tracts, counties, ZIP Codes) created by the U.S. Bureau of the Census, the U.S. Postal Service, and other agencies. Many local public and private organizations, such as school boards, police departments, and retail businesses, create boundaries for their own purposes.

What are districts used for with GIS? People use districts and other areas to help organize or subdivide a place so it can be more easily managed. Districts are often also used to summarize information about people or activities. Here are some examples:

Telephone boundaries, Collin County, Texas

- ◆ Assigning officers and summarizing weekly crimes by police beat
- ◆ Assigning sales people and summarizing quarterly revenues by sales territory
- ◆ Creating congressional districts and summarizing population and ethnic makeup
- ◆ Summarizing income and age by ZIP Code to target sales promotions

How is boundary information made available? Census and ZIP Code boundaries are available from government or private sources already in digital format, on disk, CD–ROM, or via the Internet. Locally created boundaries are generally used only by the organization that created them, although the information may be displayed as maps or on a computer during public meetings. Some local organizations may make their boundary databases available on disk or tape.

communication and understanding among committee members, parents, and the school board. Concludes Slagle, "This is one of those tools where [parents] can participate right at the beginning. They can actually see the numbers being generated." And that has helped make reaching consensus on the boundaries quicker and easier.

Workers at Cherokee Metropolitan District near Colorado Springs, Colorado, use GIS to respond to water main breaks.

7 Water and Sewer

It's 7:30 on a mild summer evening in the suburbs of Colorado Springs. Swing shift workers from the circuit board plant at the corner of Galley and Ford are just breaking for dinner. As they step outside, they hear a deep rumbling sound. The pavement in the middle of the intersection is starting to buckle. Just then, a Corvette doing about sixty reaches the intersection. It hits the bulge in the street and is airborne, all four wheels off the ground. The workers stare, mouths open. The Corvette flies through the intersection and touches down on the other side. Without even swerving, it continues on up Galley. Then the pavement breaks open and water is shooting 30 feet straight up into the air.

"That was one of our more interesting main line breaks," recalls Stuart Loosley, manager of Cherokee Metropolitan District. Loosley is responsible for the system that provides water and sewer service to about 15,000 residents in an unincorporated area on the outskirts of Colorado Springs, Colorado. The district pipes in water from wells located in a valley 19 miles to the east and stores it in a 3-million-gallon tank near the low-lying south end of the district. Powerful booster pumps send the water to two other storage tanks on hills at the district's north end. From there, the water is fed downhill to houses and other buildings.

Aside from the 10-inch lines that pump water to the big storage tanks, there isn't enough pressure in the pipes to create the geyser-like breaks similar to the one Loosley described. Most leaks are small affairs that bubble up under the sidewalk or in the middle of the street. And even those are pretty rare, occurring maybe once a month. Still, leaks do occur, most commonly, according to Field Supervisor Mark Cuchiara, when the ground shifts. That can happen a number of ways, such

Cherokee Metropolitan District provides water and sewer service to 15,000 residents. GIS helps workers maintain the district's system of pumps, tanks, and pipes.

"By the time they go see what's going on—to find out if it's a main break or something else—I can have a map for them."

Stuart Loosley, district manager

Leaks can rapidly spread underground, collapsing a street. Rebuilding and repaving a street costs money. So workers need to notify residents and begin excavating right away.

as a roadbed settling. When that happens, says Cuchiara, "the pipe just snaps like a twig."

The major concern is damage to the street. If left unchecked, a leak can spread underground. Rapidly, if it's on a hill. "And then," says Loosley, "the asphalt just collapses." Rebuilding and paving the street can be costly. So Supervisor Cuchiara and his crew want to get the water shut off and start repairs as quickly as possible. But they also want to give the residents affected by the leak some advance warning that the water will be off. "You want to give them time to gather some water for drinking or making coffee," explains Loosley, "because you never know until you get down to the leak how long it's really going to take."

Loosley uses GIS to get Cuchiara the information he and his crew need to quickly respond to a leak. When someone reports a leak to the district office, the receptionist contacts Cuchiara, or whichever crew member is on call, who heads over to find out how bad the leak is. Meanwhile, at the district office,

Loosley sits down at the computer and clicks the "Water/Wastewater" option on the district's GIS menu. A few seconds after he's typed in the address, the GIS draws a map of the block showing all the pipes and valves under the street, along with features on the surface. Each type of information is drawn in a different color so it can be easily distinguished: lot lines are red, houses are pink, curbs are black. The main water lines are thick blue lines, the water service pipes are thin blue lines, and the shutoff valve for each house is a red square. Loosley clicks another button and the GIS sends the map to the printer. A few minutes later, when Cuchiara arrives at the office, the printed map is waiting for him. He takes the map and heads back to the field, followed by the crew with the backhoe and other equipment.

Using the map, Cuchiara first locates the main valves that need to be shut off to stop the leak. Then he checks to see which houses will lose their water. The map shows him where the water service for each house reaches the curb, so he can tell which ones are connected to the broken main.

The crew notifies the affected residents that in about twenty minutes the water will be off for the next few hours. After giving the residents enough time to store some water, the crew shuts off the main valves, excavates the main, and repairs the break. About two hours later, the water is back on.

Before the district had the GIS, workers had to look through hand-drawn maps stored at the district office. Each map covered a large area, so precious time could be wasted searching for the right street and finding out which houses were affected. Even then, it might not show the most up-to-date information, since redrawing the maps by hand was a big job and done only infrequently. On top of that, the map had to stay in the office. With the GIS, says Loosley, "by the time they go up and see what's going on—to find out if it's a main break or something else—I can have a map for them." When crew members swing back by the office to pick up the equipment, they can take a detailed map with them into the field and start notifying residents rather than poring over maps at the office.

After repairs are done, Loosley enters all the information about the leak into the GIS database: the date, location, and cause of the leak;

the size of the pipe, its type, and age. "We maintain information like that on all the leaks we have in the district," he notes. Loosley can display a map based on any of this information. "That'll help us determine if there's any kind of a pattern," he explains. He can then prevent leaks by having field crews replace older pipes in an area susceptible to ground shift, for example.

Loosley recently used the GIS to create detailed 8½-by-11-inch maps of each block in the district, showing which side of the street the

Loosley enters the address where the leak was reported and the system zooms in to that street. He then creates a map to give to the repair crew showing the water main, valves, and water service for each house.

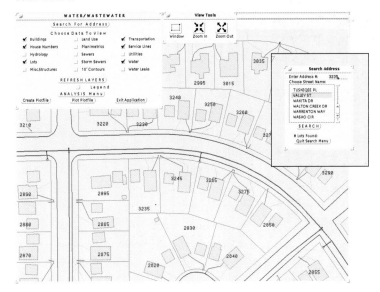

In his office, Loosley prints the map of the area surrounding the water main break.

main lines are on, how many valves are at each intersection, and where the hydrants are, among other things. A complete set of maps is kept in a notebook in each truck. "Any information in there we'll use before we dig," says Cuchiara. "If you don't know where it is, you just open that book. It's pretty handy to have right in the truck."

Cuchiara and his crew are also responsible for flushing all the sewer lines every three years. Loosley uses the GIS to keep track of the process—he can draw a map of all the sewer lines and click on any one to find out when it was last flushed. Or he can create a

The district's GIS includes a record of all the water main breaks that have occurred. Loosley can point to any leak on the map and get detailed information about it.

map showing the lines due to be flushed next, in the order they should be done so that flushing proceeds downstream. He has also used the GIS to create maps for the local fire department showing all the houses more than 250 feet from a hydrant. Firefighters can see if any of those are beyond the reach of hose extensions, and let the district know they need to add new hydrants.

Loosley realized how useful GIS would be after talking with counterparts at the City of Colorado Springs and other water districts who were already using it. In 1989, he contracted with a firm in Denver to design and build the utilities database: manholes, mains, water service, sewers, hydrants. The firm used aerial photos and field surveys to get the information and put it into the GIS. In the end, building the whole database cost $40,000. Loosley then arranged an exchange with the county's GIS department: copies of his utilities database for their parcel information. That included lot lines, street addresses, land use, and other information that the district needed for its database.

The big job now is keeping the information up to date. Loosley gets updated parcel information from the county twice a year. When new houses are built in the district, he digitizes the building footprints directly from the developers' plans. The location of new water

You can use GIS to map complex networks such as gas, water, or electric, so you can take quick action if there's a break or other interruption. Workers at Cherokee Metropolitan District in Colorado Springs, Colorado, use GIS in case of a water main break to find out which houses are connected to the main.

What they do...

1 Zoom in to the location. The district manager enters the address where the leak was reported. The GIS displays a street map of that block.

2 Draw the network features. The manager then clicks several buttons to display the critical features: the main, the valves, the building footprint of each house on the block, and the location of the water service for each. He prints the map.

3 Identify the connected features. The repair crew uses the map in the field to identify the houses that are connected to the broken main. The workers then notify residents that they are starting repairs.

All of these houses are served by this water main.

More examples of using GIS to map networks...

◆ The Energy Company of Bogota uses GIS to manage the distribution of electricity for Bogota City, Colombia. The GIS helps them monitor and control the flow of electricity through 4,500 kilometers of feeder lines connected to thirty-six substations. The system also includes thousands of transformers, poles, and switches.

◆ The Northern Kentucky Area Planning Commission used GIS to help the city of Park Hills, Kentucky, find points in the sewer network where storm water and sewage mix during periods of heavy rainfall. Those points are monitored by city engineers to make sure Park Hills meets the requirements of the Clean Water Act.

How a geographic network works...

The point where networked lines connect to each other, such as an electrical pole, is called a "node." The GIS stores a list of all the nodes and the lines that connect to each.

The GIS also knows which other features, such as transformers, switches, and meters, the lines connect to.

Since the GIS also knows the direction of flow along each

Denton, Texas, electric system

line, it can determine what is upstream and downstream from a given point in the network. If, for example, a transformer goes out, you can immediately see which houses are affected.

The GIS stores information about each feature: the type of pole or transformer, whether lines are above or underground, whether switches are open or closed. Different symbols on the map indicate what

- PAD SWITCH - OPEN
- LIGHTNING ARRESTOR
- FUSE
- CAPACITOR BANK
- AIR SWITCH - CLOSED
- AIR SWITCH - OPEN
- ELECTRIC MANHOLE
- PULL BOX
- PEDESTAL
- FAULT INDICATOR
- ELECTRIC METER
- OVERHEAD PRIMARY CONDUCTOR
- UNDERGROUND PRIMARY CONDUCTOR
- OVERHEAD SECONDARY CONDUCTOR

each feature is. There may be additional information for each feature, such as the last date a pole was serviced. The information can be displayed by simply clicking on it.

"We'll locate the main before we do any digging. If you don't know where it is, you just open the map book. It's pretty handy to have right in the truck."

MARK CUCHIARA, FOREMAN

service lines comes from measurements the field crew makes when they go out to inspect the new lines. Loosley then draws the lines directly in the GIS.

With all his other duties, Loosley is hard pressed to find time to enter new data into the GIS. "My crews are after me to get them maps of the new areas," he grins. So he is training others to use the system as well. And the system now has so much information in it that creating and drawing the maps is not as fast as Loosley would like. So he's hoping to get a faster computer to keep up with all the uses for the GIS.

GIS is not the only computer technology the district uses. Another system monitors the water level in the tanks and automatically turns wells and pumps on and off. And when they read the meters, crews use handheld computers to enter and calculate water usage. But it's the GIS that helps Loosley and Cuchiara maintain the network of pipes and valves that delivers the water to people's homes. Water is one of the basic services that people usually don't think about until it's not there. The district's GIS helps make sure the water keeps flowing.

Creating meter-reading routes in Seattle, Washington

Seattle City Light uses GIS to create route maps for their meter readers. Previously, meter readers relied on maps that were out of date by as much as twenty years and difficult to read. Using GIS, Seattle City Light can generate new maps that are easier to read and maintain. The route boundaries are created by matching customer account information to a GIS database of streets. The boundary areas are drawn on the map in different colors to distinguish the routes from each other. The maps also include route numbers, street names, and block addresses for reference.

Locating storm sewer problems in Cincinnati, Ohio

The Metropolitan Sewer District of Greater Cincinnati uses GIS to locate trouble spots in the storm sewer network by tracking complaints after a heavy rain. By mapping the relationship between complaints and amount of rainfall, they can see where to focus preventive maintenance efforts—keeping sewers free of debris, for instance. "This spatial analysis could not be feasibly performed by any other means than GIS," says Dr. Michael Sweeney, the district's deputy director. Sweeney also uses GIS on a laptop computer to present the information to citizens at community meetings.

building footprint

A building footprint is the outline a building makes on the ground. Building footprints are often used on maps to show where the building is located in relation to other features such as curbs, lot lines, water and sewer lines, and other buildings. Building footprints are common in GIS databases used by utility companies, property tax assessors, police, and fire departments.

What's in a utility database? A utility database contains the objects that make up the network of that utility: pipes, valves, and meters for a water utility; wires, transformers, poles, and meters for an electric utility; and so on. The database also contains information about the characteristics of each of the objects.

Where does utility data come from? Traditionally, utility companies have used paper maps to show where objects in the network are. These maps are digitized or scanned and added to the GIS database. Utilities also use aerial photography to get the location of objects in the network that are above ground—manhole covers, valve covers, hydrants, street lights, utility poles, and so on—and then digitize that information into the GIS. Information about the objects is kept in tables and databases. The GIS is used to link this information to the digital maps.

What can a GIS utility database be used for? Anything having to do with managing the flow through a network. Here are a few examples:

United Illuminating power network, New Haven, Connecticut

◆ Tracing through an electrical grid to find the source of a power outage

◆ Monitoring the condition of pipes in a natural gas pipeline

◆ Keeping track of scheduled flushings of sewers

◆ Designing the layout of fiber-optic cables for a telecommunication system

Who uses the utility information? Utility databases are mainly used by the private companies and public utility districts that provide the utility service. These organizations may exchange data with each other and with local government agencies. When they work with a common set of information, the organizations can be more efficient when planning, performing maintenance, and responding to emergencies. Many communities also use a GIS utility database for the One Call or DigSafe telephone numbers that homeowners or construction crews call to find out where the utility lines are before they dig.

Solid waste planners at

Portland's regional

planning agency, Metro,

use GIS to evaluate their

recycling programs.

8 Recycling

Wearing white protective jumpsuits, four workers wait silently at the Metro South waste transfer station on the outskirts of Portland, Oregon. A gray drizzle falls as the mountain of trash, deposited all morning by garbage trucks, grows. Soon, the truck they've been watching for, fresh from its neighborhood collection route, pulls in front of them and dumps its load. A yellow Bobcat starts leveling out the trash.

One of the workers marks out a 4-by-4-foot square, using stakes and string. The crew start picking through garbage with gloved hands, putting each kind of trash into separate piles: rotting food, newspaper and junk mail, plastic, glass bottles and jars, metal cans, leaves and other yard waste. Finally they reach bare ground—the dirty job is finished. The Bobcat hauls the piles over to the scales and weighs them. This sample was worse than most—over half of it yard debris.

Keith Massie, a solid waste planner for Portland's regional planning agency, Metro, recalls those samples, taken in the late 1980s to find out what was headed for landfills. "We'd pull a truck off route and dig through the garbage," explains Massie. "We weighed the yard debris, we weighed the recyclables." The agency found that in 1987 over a quarter of the trash collected in the region was yard debris. This included just about anything people culled from their gardens and yards: grass clippings, leaves, hedge trimmings, branches, and stumps.

In Portland, the major cost of disposal is getting the trash to the landfills. Garbage trucks haul the waste to one of two transfer stations that serve the whole region. There it's loaded on trucks and hauled about 150 miles up the Columbia River Gorge to landfills in eastern Oregon. All this costs money. So the more waste that people can keep out of the

In the late 1980s, Portland Metro did a series of studies to find out how much recyclable material was being sent to landfills.

landfills, the lower the disposal costs will be. It will mean less money spent on opening and operating new transfer stations and, in the long run, fewer new landfills.

When planners at Metro found out how much yard debris was being hauled to landfills, they made it a target of the region's waste reduction efforts. Yard debris is relatively easy to recycle—it's often produced in large quantities and is uncontaminated by other garbage. Local processors use grinders to turn it into mulch and wood chips. But if left to decompose in landfills, yard debris creates gasses that have to be captured and treated. The bottom line, according to Massie: "We wanted to get yard debris out of the garbage can."

With a depot system, residents haul yard debris to recycling centers where it's turned into mulch and wood chips.

The key was making sure all households had an easy way to recycle the yard waste. It was up to each of the twenty-four cities and three counties in the region to come up with their own program. Many decided on weekly or bi-weekly curbside pickup. Private companies would haul the yard debris to processing facilities to be turned into compost and sold. Local officials did not make the decisions lightly. With curbside pickup, waste haulers would have to buy new trucks and hire new workers. Some of the cost would get passed on to the residents as part of their monthly trash collection bill.

In Washington County, officials decided to rely on depots rather than curbside pickup—residents would haul yard debris to the depots themselves. As Massie points out, "Obviously the cheapest way to do it—you don't have to raise the rates." Lynne Storz, Washington County's solid waste management coordinator, concurs that keeping trash collection rates low was an issue. "We need to cover the cost of the new services in our rates. We don't subsidize them," she says.

But while it held down collection rates, Washington County's plan also had to be as effective as curbside pickup in keeping yard debris out of the landfills. That meant most households had to be within a short drive of a depot. "A fifteen-minute travel time was the

"There is a really good acceptance of the GIS. The decision makers have a lot of trust and confidence in the system."

KEITH MASSIE, METRO SOLID WASTE PLANNER

most we figured they would go," explains Storz. So the county's solid waste planners took a paper map, located the five proposed depots, and drew a circle with a radius of 4 miles around each one. They estimated that a 4-mile radius would roughly include the area within a fifteen-minute drive. The circles they drew covered the most populous areas in the county—it looked like most households were near a depot. So in 1990 the plan went into operation.

County officials had projected that in 1992 over 14,000 tons of yard debris would be recycled at the depots as residents became aware of the system. But they were disappointed to find that only 10,600 tons were hauled to the depots that year. This was much less, per household, than the curbside pickup programs were collecting.

Steve Kraten, a planner in Metro's Recycling Section at the time, had the job of helping Washington County evaluate their yard debris recycling efforts. Recalls Storz, "What we were trying to do is say, 'x number of

people probably use these depots.' But there was no good information."

So Kraten and Massie used Metro's GIS to get the information. Recalls Kraten, "I knew about our mapping capability. I thought it's a reasonable assumption that people will take yard debris to the nearest depot. So I asked Keith to develop a map showing the travel time." In the four years since the planners at Washington County had drawn the circles on their paper map, Metro had added detailed information on streets to their GIS. So instead

Siting a new landfill in Loudoun County, Virginia

The Loudoun County Department of Natural Resources used GIS to find potential sites for a new landfill. They combined maps of such factors as slope, soils, depth to bedrock, depth to groundwater, and distance from historic districts, main roads, and towns. The final map pinpointed about a dozen possible sites that warranted further study.

of using a 4-mile radius from each depot, Massie was able to use actual travel time along the streets.

Massie displayed a map of streets for Washington County on the screen and had the GIS calculate all the streets within a fifteen-minute drive of each depot. The GIS drew the streets for each depot using a different color. Massie drew a line around each set of streets, to define the area served by each depot. He then had the GIS shade each area a different color so it was easy to tell them apart.

Kraten wanted to see how these fifteen-minute drive time areas compared to the circles the county's planners had originally used. So with the colored travel time areas still on the screen, Massie had the GIS draw a circle with a 4-mile radius around each depot.

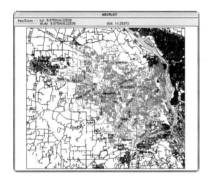

Streets within a fifteen-minute drive of Beaverton yard debris depot.

Massie had the GIS draw all the streets within a fifteen-minute drive of each depot. He then drew boundaries to create a map showing the area served by each depot. He also drew the 4-mile radius around each depot, for comparison.

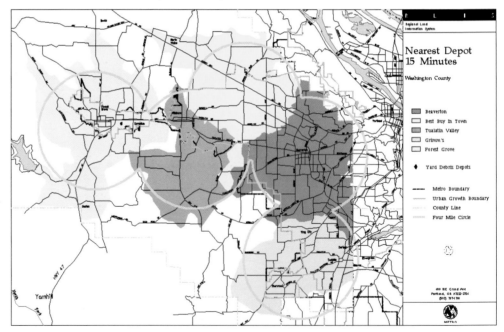

Creating garbage truck routes in Philadelphia, Pennsylvania

The City of Philadelphia uses GIS to create route maps for their garbage truck drivers. The routes take into account the speed and tonnage of garbage trucks, the width of streets, the volume of trash a building generates, and so forth. Using the new routes, the city has been able to use eighteen trucks to collect the amount of trash that used to take twenty-three. The freed-up crew has been put to work cleaning underpasses and making pickups of such bulk items as old refrigerators.

It turned out there were several densely populated areas that—while within the circles—weren't actually within a fifteen-minute drive of any of the depots. That could partly account for the lower than expected amount of recycled yard debris. Since the new analysis used travel time along streets it gave a more precise view of which areas were and were not being served by the depots. Says Kraten, "It was pretty convincing evidence."

The next step was to figure out the actual number of households within each depot's service area. Massie overlaid the depot service areas with census block boundaries. That told him which census blocks were within each depot's service area. Since the GIS stored the number of households in each block, it was easy to total the number of households served by each depot. "One thing that became clear," says Kraten, "was that one particular depot, the Beaverton Depot, served the majority of households. And yet that depot was open only once a month."

The maps and numbers helped convince Washington County officials that they needed to either make changes in the depot system or switch to curbside pickup if they were to meet their recycling goals. After weighing the options, county officials decided to start a weekly curbside collection program for most of the county.

HOUSEHOLDS SERVED BY NEAREST DEPOT			
Nearest Depot	Single Family Households, 1990 Census	Additional Through 12/31/92	Total No. Single Family Households
Beaverton	39,310	1,864	41,174
Grimm's	9,239	958	10,197
Best Buy in Town	13,056	1,557	14,613
Tualatin Valley	6,104	181	6,285
Forest Grove	5,436	169	5,605
Totals	73,145	4,729	77,874

You can use GIS to find the area within a given distance or travel time of a location. You can then find out who or what is in that area. Planners at Portland Metro measured travel time along streets to find out how many people were within a fifteen-minute drive of yard debris recycling depots so they could estimate how many people were likely to use them.

What they did...

1 **Assigned an average travel time to each street.** The planners started by having the GIS calculate the average time needed to drive each street segment, from intersection to intersection. They first assigned each segment an average travel time value, based on its type—local residential, major thoroughfare, and so on. The GIS multiplied the street length by the travel time value to get the time needed to drive each particular segment. For example, a residential street might be driven at 30 m.p.h., on average. That converts to two minutes per mile. If a block is one-tenth of a mile long, it would take .2 minutes to drive the length of that block.

2 **Found the streets within the specified travel time.** The GIS started at the inter-section nearest the recycling depot, the "origin," and worked outward. At each intersection it checked the street segments in all directions and tagged them if the cumulative travel time from the origin was less than the limit (fifteen minutes in this example). It continued until all street segments within fifteen minutes of the origin had been tagged. The GIS worked outward from all depots simultaneously. That way streets were always allocated to the closest depot.

3 **Created the travel time boundaries.** Once the GIS had tagged the streets within fifteen minutes of each depot, the planners drew boundaries to enclose the area covered by the tagged streets surrounding each depot.

4 **Overlaid the boundaries with other data.** The planners then used the GIS to overlay the travel time boundaries with census information to find the number of households within fifteen minutes of each depot.

Other ways of finding the distance from a location...

Instead of travel time, you can use actual mileage along the streets. Travel time varies based on speed limit, time of day, and other factors, but mileage is constant. Another way of finding 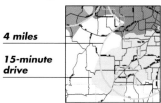 the distance from a location is to have the GIS draw a circle around the location. You specify the radius of the circle. This method is quicker, but less exact, than using mileage or travel time along streets.

4 miles

15-minute drive

More examples of using GIS to find what's within a given distance...

◆ The City of Las Vegas, Nevada, used GIS to map the area within a three-minute response time of each fire station. The map clearly showed which areas of the city were well covered by the existing stations and which areas might benefit from a new one.

◆ The City of Newton, Massachusetts, used GIS to map an area of 1,000 feet around each school to create "drug-free zones." People dealing drugs within the zone may be subject to additional sanctions. Each arrest is mapped to see if it was made within the 1,000-foot zone.

Massie has also used the GIS to manage the disposal of hazardous waste. Household hazardous waste, such as paint, weed killer, and car batteries, has to be disposed of properly to keep the soil and water clean. So Metro's planners schedule day-long drop-off "events" at different locations around the region. Massie uses the GIS to show the areas within five, ten, and fifteen minutes of each event. Using the maps, planners can see whether they need to schedule additional events at other locations to make sure the entire region is covered.

The GIS can do this analysis because it can calculate the time needed to travel each street segment, from intersection to intersection. Since the GIS knows which streets connect at each intersection, it adds the travel time in all directions out from a location until it reaches the limit.

The street data for the analysis came initially from the U.S. Bureau of the Census. Planners at Metro then hired a private firm to find and correct errors in the locations of streets, and to add the street type and travel time information. That work was completed in 1992. Now the three counties in the region provide Metro with information on new streets several times a year so the GIS database stays current.

The solid waste department is just one of the groups at Metro using GIS. Transportation planners use it to plan the location of light rail tracks and stations. And the regional planning department uses GIS to provide information to politicians and the public on the current and future growth of the region.

"There is a really good acceptance of the GIS," says Massie. "The decision makers have a lot of trust and confidence in the system." Massie admits that with the yard waste analysis "there's still a little bit of yard debris in the garbage can. But it's a fraction of what it was."

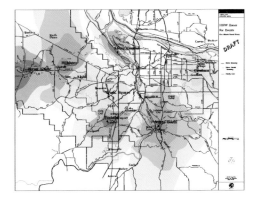

Massie uses the GIS to find out how many residents are within five, ten, and fifteen minutes of household hazardous waste drop-off events. Planners use the information to see if they need to schedule additional events.

WORKING WITH STREET DATA

What's in a street database? A city or
county street database consists of street centerlines and the intersections, or nodes, where
streets cross or meet. The centerlines and intersections show where streets are located and how
they're connected. The database also includes
information about each street.

Where does street data come from? Many city and county engineering
departments have surveyed their streets and store this data in a CAD system. This
data can also be used by a GIS. Some counties have created street databases
from their parcel databases by drafting and digitizing the street centerlines. The
U.S. Bureau of the Census has also created a nationwide database of streets with
addresses. Many local agencies start with this data and update it using locally
collected information on address ranges, street types, traffic flow, and so on.

What can a GIS street database be used for?

**Managing traffic
flow in Stockton,
California**

◆ Creating and updating street maps

◆ Scheduling and tracking street maintenance

◆ Dispatching and routing emergency vehicles

◆ Managing traffic flow

◆ Creating bus routes

◆ Routing delivery trucks

How is street data made available? The U.S. Bureau of the Census sells its
street files, known as TIGER/Line files, on CD-ROM. Many libraries also have the
TIGER/Line CDs for their state. A number of private companies sell corrected and
updated versions of the Census Bureau streets. Some local and regional governments also sell street databases they've created.

TIGER/Line

TIGER/Line is the geographic data the U.S.
Bureau of the Census uses in conducting
the census. It includes streets and addresses, census tracts, city and county
boundaries, and more. TIGER/Line data can
be converted into a format readable by a
GIS and used for many types of analysis
and mapping. The data is sold by the Census Bureau on CD-ROM, as well as by private vendors who have enhanced the data
with additional information. TIGER is an
acronym for Topologically Integrated Geographic Encoding and Referencing system.

Market researchers and real estate agents at Star Enterprise in Atlanta, Georgia, use GIS to find the best sites to build new Texaco gas stations.

9 Business

Atlanta, Georgia, 1956. A white Cadillac convertible pulls up under the narrow awning that hovers above the two pumps. "Fill 'er up with Fire Chief!" the woman calls over her shoulder, as she strolls over to get a Coca-Cola out of the ice box. The attendant in his brown cap with the red and white star scurries around to the back and opens the gas cap. "Check your oil?" he asks while wiping the windshield. He shuts the hood, checks the tires, and replaces the nozzle on the pump. "That'll be $4.50, ma'am." She opens her shiny white plastic purse and pulls out a five-dollar bill. "Keep the change," she smiles as she drives off.

Suburban Atlanta, forty years later. A dusty white Honda Accord pulls up to the tall pump displaying the red and white star. A woman wearing black pants and a white tank top hops out and slips her Texaco card into the slot. Banks of bright lights shine down from the massive canopy overhead as she fills the tank with CleanSystem3. When she's done, she drops the Accord off at the car wash and strolls over to the Star 21 food mart. She grabs a carton of lowfat milk off the shelf and a chicken sandwich from the fast-food express at the back of the store. Then she jumps back into her clean car and heads for home.

The neighborhood gas station of the 1990s is a far cry from the little white, boxy stations of the 1950s. But it's still a fixture on corners across America. And it's still a big part of Texaco's business. Today's stations try to lure customers with speed and convenience. Most feature electronic pumps, a food mart, a fast-food outlet, and often a car wash or quick lube. But these modern stations don't come cheap—each one costs Texaco about $1.5 million to open. Finding a good location is the key to building a station that will bring in the customers and turn a profit.

The neighborhood gas station has always been an important part of Texaco's business.

Frank Herbst is manager of assets for Star Enterprise, a joint venture between Texaco and Saudi Aramco that builds and runs many of Texaco's gas stations in eastern and Gulf Coast states. Herbst has been with Star since the company formed in 1989, and was with Texaco for nineteen years before that. He knows well what's involved in picking the right location for a new station—finding the neighborhoods where potential customers are, looking at traffic volume for each intersection, and sizing up the competition. The search takes time. And in fast-growing suburban areas, there are a lot of other companies also trying to find those same good sites.

In the early 1990s, Richard Arold, manager of the Brand Management group at Star Enterprise, began looking for a computer system that would accelerate the process of finding good sites. By 1994, Arold's group had developed a GIS-based system called STARFIRES (Star Fully Integrated Retail Evaluation System). When the company decides to open a new station, Todd Kroh, coordinator of modeling in the Brand Management department, uses STARFIRES to help Herbst and the real estate agents at Star find the best sites. "STARFIRES," explains Herbst, "can zero in on the areas surrounding a city that have the highest concentrations of our targeted segments and then pull

A modern station costs Texaco about $1.5 million to open, so the company wants to make sure they build new stations in locations that will attract a lot of customers.

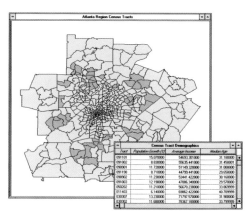

Kroh uses STARFIRES to find all the census tracts in the region that meet his demographic criteria.

it down to specific corners that have high traffic counts."

One such city is fast-growing Atlanta. At his computer, Kroh begins his task by displaying a map of all the census tracts in the twelve-county area surrounding the city. He specifies the characteristics of the customers he's looking for—age, income, and so forth. The tracts also have to meet certain minimum requirements—in population density and growth rate, for example. The system finds all the census tracts that meet the criteria Kroh specified and shades them purple. He sees there are several in Gwinnett County. It's just the kind of area the company is looking for: the population has doubled every ten years since 1960, the median income is over $45,000, and the average commute time to work is higher than the state average.

Kroh has STARFIRES find the intersections within each of the selected tracts that have a high daily traffic count, say 15,000 cars or more. It marks each of those with a red dot and prints out a list of them. Herbst's field agents use that list to visit each intersection. They come back with a list of sites that are the right size and available for purchase.

Kroh then locates each site in the system and draws a 3-mile radius around it, the typical trade area for a neighborhood station. He gets the specific demographic data for the area and enters it, along with the traffic data, into a computer model. He also enters in the specs for the station—its dimensions, the number of pumps, whether there will be a convenience store, and so on. Once he plugs in all the data,

the model gives him a projected sales volume for that station, in gallons of gas a month. He then has the system draw a yellow dot at the location of each competing gas station. Kroh measures the distance from the proposed station to any competing stations within the 3-mile radius. Using that distance, along with information about the competitors, he calculates how much each competing station might cut into the sales of the proposed station.

The numbers and maps go back to Herbst and his real estate staff, as well as to the business unit manager and to the regional sales manager for the area. They analyze the results of the model based on their own knowledge of the industry. "We apply some business logic to what the model is telling us," explains Herbst. "If we don't see what the model is seeing, we may modify the forecasts." Herbst

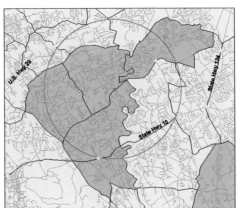

STARFIRES finds intersections within the selected tracts that have daily traffic counts higher than 15,000. Kroh then draws a 3-mile radius around each potential site and analyzes the competition (yellow dots) within that trade area.

> *"STARFIRES gives us a scientific way to determine the best sites for our stores. We can find the areas that we want to focus on and be assured of finding some pretty good properties."*
>
> **TODD KROH, COMPUTER MODELING COORDINATOR**

sends a complete proposal to top management for final approval. He and his staff then work up the final cost estimate and put the project out for bid. Six months later, the new station is open for business.

At that point, Herbst and Kroh start tracking the performance of the station to see if the sales projections from STARFIRES match the actual volume of gas sold. If there's a big difference, "we'll try to identify what's happening in this station that perhaps we didn't pick up in the model," explains Herbst. They put that information back into the model, so the next time it'll give them even more accurate results.

Before the development of STARFIRES, Star Enterprise real estate agents would spend a lot of time on the road looking for potential sites. They'd size up each neighborhood and estimate whether a station would do well there. Sometimes they'd go to the local transportation agency and spend even more time digging through lists of traffic counts, looking for corners that met the criteria. And they still didn't know how many potential customers lived in the vicinity. Now detailed information on customers, traffic volume, and competitors is all in one place. As Kroh explains, "We can find the areas that we want to focus on and be assured of finding some pretty good properties." Herbst concurs. "It really reduces our search time for prime locations," he says. And when Herbst is ready to put together the package to send to top management, the system prints out the maps he needs, with the sales volume and other information right on them.

Marketing bank services in Ardmore, Oklahoma

Sales managers at Lincoln Bank in Ardmore, Oklahoma, use GIS to help market the bank's services. They map customer locations with census demographic information to decide which areas to focus on for selling home loans, Certificates of Deposit, and other products. Using GIS helps the bank find neighborhoods that meet certain criteria, such as a high level of home ownership or a specific income range. The bank officers also use GIS to show they are meeting federal guidelines by making loans available to all customers within the bank's market area.

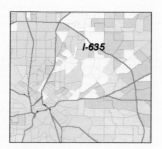

You can use GIS to search for a site, a building, or other geographic feature. The GIS can quickly look at many features and select just those that have the characteristics you're looking for. Analysts at Star Enterprise in Atlanta, Georgia, use GIS to find the best intersections for building new gas stations.

What they do...

1 Decide what makes a good site.
The analysts first set the requirements for the site. Good sites are at busy intersections in neighborhoods that have many potential customers and few nearby competitors.

2 Start the search.
The analysts use the GIS to find the neighborhoods where there are likely to be lots of customers that match the company's customer profiles.

3 Narrow the search.
Next they use the GIS to identify the intersections in the selected neighborhoods that have high traffic counts and few competitors nearby.

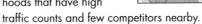

4 Make the decision.
The analysts calculate the projected sales at each intersection, based on where each is in relation to customers and competitors. They identify the best intersections. The real estate agents then look at individual lots at each intersection to decide on the final sites.

Using GIS to search...

A GIS can help you find what you're looking for because it

- combines many different features in one system (e.g., census tracts, street intersections, gas stations)

- includes both the locations of the features and their characteristics

- has the capability to search based on location (e.g., which intersections are within this census tract) and based on characteristics (e.g., which intersections have a traffic count greater than 15,000).

More examples of using GIS to search for a site...

- The Charlotte, North Carolina, YMCA used GIS to help decide where to open a new branch. They mapped population, employment, and income information to compare two possible sites. They also mapped the locations of all their members to see how much the proposed sites would cut into membership at their existing branches.

- The Orange County Transportation Authority in Orange, California, used GIS to help find sites for park-and-ride lots. They mapped information such as population density, employment, traffic volume, and land use to find available parcels near freeways in areas where many long-distance commuters live.

Kroh and the other analysts use STARFIRES to create customer profiles of each station, so the shelves in the food mart can be stocked with products that will appeal to the clientele.

Before, the agents would place dots on paper maps and write the information out by hand. "All that's now generated from STARFIRES," notes Herbst.

Kroh gets all the data for STARFIRES from private companies that compile the information from census data, sales records, customer surveys, and other sources. Kroh is considering adding land parcel data to the system as well. That way, when he creates a list of target intersections, he'll also be able to create a list of the parcels at each corner showing the size of each, its assessed value, its owner, current zoning, and other information. That will further reduce the time field staff have to spend doing research.

Currently, Kroh is setting up the system to run on a laptop computer, so the agents can do the analysis themselves, right in the field. They'll be able to forecast sales volume for a potential site or decide if an existing station is worth renovating.

Kroh and the other analysts at Star Enterprise also use the system to study existing gas stations. Using the demographic information, along with customer surveys conducted at the stations, they can find out, for example, whether people in the neighborhood are likelier to pick up denture cream at the food mart, or diapers. Store managers can then stock the shelves accordingly. The information also helps Star Enterprise decide which fast-food chains to put in the stations. "We can determine which food product, such as pizza, submarine sandwiches, chicken, or tacos, would sell best at each site," says Kroh.

Kroh and Herbst know the computer doesn't have all the answers. "We use the model very much as a tool—we don't use it as a given," says Herbst. But he admits, "It's been giving

Finding houses for sale in Broomfield, Colorado

RAM Realty of Broomfield, Colorado, uses GIS to help locate homes and commercial properties for its clients. Using a GIS available to real estate agents over the Internet, broker Bob Most can create custom maps for each client, showing properties for sale in the right price range, along with other information such as the locations of schools, parks, and shopping centers. He can also generate reports that describe the neighborhoods. The system has information for the entire country, so Most can create maps for his clients moving to other parts of the state, or even to other regions. Having all the information in one place saves Most time and money. It also helps his clients. "Certainly it's a benefit for the buyers and sellers," he says. "With the information that we can give them they can be well armed to make the right decisions."

us pretty decent results." Kroh backs that up. "STARFIRES gives us a scientific way to determine the best sites for our stores," he says. And that means going where the customers are. Herbst smiles as he sums it up: "We think it might give us a little competitive advantage."

census tract

Census tracts are the basic areas used by the U.S. Bureau of the Census to store information about the population. While information is collected about the individual households in each census tract, it's available only as summary data (for example, the average income of all the households in the census tract). Every census tract has roughly the same number of people (the average size in 1990 was 4,000 people). So in densely populated places tracts are small, while in more rural places they can cover a large area. Because so much information is collected about the people who live within them—information on age, income, ethnicity, education, and much more— census tracts are used for many different purposes, from redistricting voting precincts to targeting areas for special sales promotions.

What is demographic data? Demographic data is information about people, commonly including age, education level, ethnic background, employment, and income. It can also include things like health statistics, buying preferences, and television viewing habits. While the data is collected about individuals or households, it is usually summarized by area, such as census tract or ZIP Code, to show the patterns within a place.

Where does demographic data come from? In the United States, the primary source of demographic data is the census, conducted every ten years by the U.S. Bureau of the Census. Several hundred pieces of information about each household were collected during the 1990 census. To store and summarize the information, the Census Bureau subdivides counties into census tracts and subdivides census tracts into block groups. These areas, along with ZIP Codes, have become the standard for summarizing many types of demographic information. In addition to the census, universities, private companies, and other government agencies collect demographic data of all kinds from surveys, sales records, licenses and registrations, and other records.

What is demographic data used for with GIS? Anything having to do with knowing who lives where. Here are just a few uses:
- Finding out how many people live in an area, in case of an earthquake or other emergency
- Deciding which newspapers or magazines to place ads in
- Identifying where to allocate more services, such as health care facilities
- Figuring out the best place to build a new store or restaurant
- Tracking how the population in a place is changing so services can be planned, such as where and when new sewage treatment plants will be needed

How is demographic information made available? Much demographic data is available in digital form on disk, CD–ROM, or via the Internet, from government or private sources. In most cases, the appropriate boundary data is distributed along with the demographic data, also in a form readable by a GIS. The U.S. Bureau of the Census World Wide Web site lets you look at summary information and create custom maps online.

Students at Cass Technical High School in Detroit

used GIS to alert children and parents about the

health risks of lead in drinking water.

10 Public Health

Four high school students stand on the auditorium stage at Bennett Elementary in southwest Detroit, a map of the city projected onto a giant pull-down screen behind them. The entire school has turned out for this mid-morning assembly, and a low din fills the room as the teenagers introduce themselves. "Now we're going to show you a short video," 11th-grader Janelle Jenkins announces from the stage. The lights go down, and the screen fills with an image of water running from a kitchen tap. "Do you ever think about the water in your faucet?" Jenkins asks in the voice-over. "Is it dangerous? Could it hurt you? It could...if it has lead in it." The room falls silent as all eyes focus on the screen.

Bennett Elementary was just one of the many Detroit schools that Jenkins and her three classmates, Bryce Anderson-Small, Adrienne Lewis, and David Sheikhnejad, visited in 1994 to let kids know how unhealthy lead in drinking water could be. The video they made, called "Getting the Lead Out," was part of a project to help the City of Detroit increase public awareness about the problem.

"It's important for everyone to realize that lead in drinking water is a serious health hazard," says Jenkins. Randy Raymond, the students' science teacher at Cass Technical High School, explains: "From 10:00 at night to 6:00 in the morning, the water's standing in the pipes and it accumulates the lead. If you have 120 feet of lead pipe in the ground, 1-inch diameter, you've got about 14 liters of lead-tainted water." Children under twelve, since they're growing fast and can absorb lead more rapidly into the bloodstream, are particularly at risk. The long-term effects can be severe, including learning disabilities, decreased growth, impaired hearing, and even brain damage. Luckily, there's an easy solution. "The problems can

Cass Technical High School, located in downtown Detroit, is the largest high school in Michigan. Students compete to enter one of twenty-two programs offered at the school, from science to performing arts.

"It's important for everyone to realize that lead in drinking water is a serious health hazard."

JANELLE JENKINS, STUDENT

be avoided," notes Jenkins, "by simply flushing the lead out of the system before drinking the water." All it takes is flushing the toilet a couple of times first thing in the morning to bring fresh water into the house.

In 1986, a nationwide ban restricted the use of lead pipe for drinking water supply. And while new construction has not used lead pipe in Detroit since that time, many homes in the city still have lead pipe. The water department had been putting warnings in with the water bills. But the city couldn't be sure everyone was reading the notices. And in the many cases where landlords paid those bills, the tenants would never see them. So in the early 1990s, the City of Detroit Department of Water and Sewer contracted a local engineering firm and the University of Michigan School of Public Health to find out just how many homes still had lead pipe and to come up with ways to reduce the risk to the city's children.

The engineers went into the field and found almost 200,000 homes in the city with lead pipe. Replacing it all would cost $300-$400 million,

money the city just didn't have. So the researchers at the university decided the best approach would be to step up the public awareness campaign, by going directly to schools and community groups. The city wanted to find out where there were clusters of homes with lead pipe, so it could start by focusing its efforts in those neighborhoods. But trying to map the locations of all 200,000 homes by hand was not feasible—the task was just too big. And, at that time, neither the Department of Water and Sewer, the engineering firm, nor the School of Public Health had the GIS capability that was required to do the job.

One of the professors involved in the study knew that Raymond and his students at Cass Tech had been using GIS to study other environmental health issues. He asked them to help find out which neighborhoods were most at risk. Raymond's students entered the addresses of the homes into a computer database, which they linked to a map of streets stored in the GIS. That allowed them to show the locations of all the homes with

Raymond's students entered the addresses of the homes into a computer database, which they linked to a map of streets stored in the GIS. That allowed them to show the locations of all the homes with lead pipe.

lead pipe, information city officials had never seen mapped before. "They never had really considered that they could put it on a map and begin to look at it," Raymond says.

Armed with this information, the city began the public awareness campaign. Jenkins and the other students pitched in. They set to work getting articles in the paper and making the video to show to elementary schools and community groups. "We created a significant interest in the community," says Raymond. "Neighborhood groups began contacting the kids, wanting specific information on how to know whether you have lead pipe in your house, and what you should do about it."

But the students didn't stop there. Jenkins also wanted to see if they could find any relationship between lead pipe water service and student test scores, to see what effect the lead-tainted water had on the learning ability of the city's children. She started by using the GIS to create a map showing census block groups with high numbers of elementary school children. She then mapped median household income, average age of house, and other census information, to identify neighborhoods that were similar to each other except for the number of homes with lead pipe. That would help make sure the test scores weren't overly influenced by factors other than exposure to lead. Using the maps,

Jenkins chose three study areas. Next she mapped the locations of elementary schools within the three areas and assigned each a risk level—high, medium, or low—based on the number of homes with lead pipe near each school. Finally, she looked at fifth-grade standardized achievement test scores to see if the high-risk schools had lower test scores. (Fifth

Jenkins used GIS to explore the relationship between lead pipe water service and student test scores. She mapped census information to select three study areas and then mapped the location of elementary schools in those areas in relation to homes with lead pipe.

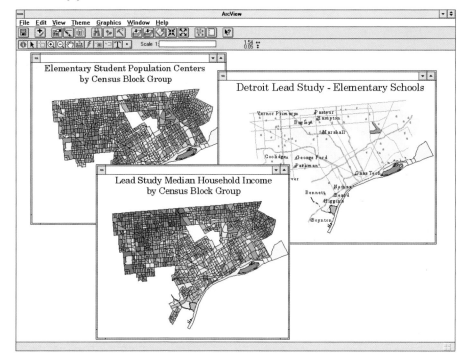

grade, as Raymond points out, "is about the time IQ stabilizes.")

But no clear pattern emerged. In any given year, test scores from high-risk schools were no different from scores at low-risk schools. "We didn't find the kind of results that we were hoping for with the test score information," admits Raymond. He concludes that the data they had did not support the detailed analysis they were trying to do. To protect the elementary students' privacy, the school district did not release test scores for individual students, only average test scores for each school. Without that data, it wasn't possible to relate student performance to lead exposure on a one-to-one basis.

In the end, though, the GIS study helped create better public awareness of the problem, which was, after all, the main goal of the project. Without the GIS, the students would not have been able to carry out a study of this magnitude. And the city would not have gotten the maps it needed.

Because of their work on the lead pipe study, Raymond and several of his students were recently asked by the university's School of Public Health to work on a new study funded by the United States Centers for Disease Control and Prevention. "We're using GIS to do all of the data analysis," says Raymond. The goal of the study is to compare maternal and infant care in two low-income neighborhoods in Detroit—one on the east side, a predominantly African-American community, and another on the southwest side, comprised mostly of Latino families.

census block group

Census block groups are the smallest geographic area for which the U.S. Bureau of the Census stores summary census information. In the 1990 census, block groups generally contained between 250 and 550 households. The demographic information available for block groups is much the same as that available for census tracts. Since block groups provide information about a smaller geographic area than census tracts, you can use them to do more detailed analysis.

Measuring the benefits of trees in Atlanta, Georgia

American Forests, a nonprofit organization based in Washington, D.C., uses GIS to measure the economic benefits of trees growing in cities. For the City of Atlanta, they found the summer energy savings from trees shading homes to be about $4.6 million annually citywide. The trees also reduce stormwater runoff by about 35 percent, saving the city from having to build additional stormwater management facilities costing millions of dollars. Cities use the program developed by American Forests to predict the costs and benefits of planting or removing trees.

You can use GIS to help you see geographic patterns in your data. That can help you decide which areas to focus on for some action, such as a redevelopment effort or an advertising campaign. You can also see whether there is a relationship, such as cause and effect, between things based on their location. Students at Cass Technical High School in Detroit used GIS to see if they could find a relationship between student test scores and the location of houses with lead pipe water service.

Another example of using GIS to look for patterns...

Students at the University of South Florida used GIS to map the locations of banks and grocery stores in Tampa in relation to the African-American population of the city. The maps were part of a study to see if the minority population had the same access to basic goods and services as other residents of the city.

What they did...

1 Defined the problem. The students wanted to measure how lead in the blood affected children's ability to learn. They decided to identify neighborhoods that had many houses with lead pipe water service and see if schools near those neighborhoods reported lower than average student test scores.

2 Selected the test areas. The students used GIS to select three neighborhoods that had a high number of elementary school students and were similar except for the number of houses with lead pipe.

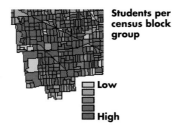

Students per census block group

Low

High

3 Plotted the maps. They then used GIS to find the elementary schools near those neighborhoods, and displayed the test scores for each. The study helped reveal which neighborhoods were at high risk, which allowed the city to target its public awareness campaign.

Schools and homes with lead pipe

Ways to map patterns...

One way to look for patterns is to use standard boundaries, such as census tracts, census block groups, or ZIP Codes. Then it's easy to create a series of maps to compare different characteristics.

Another way is to display different types of features on the same map. The GIS lets you select just the features you want. In the early 1990s, the New Jersey Department of Environmental Protection looked for census tracts that had both a large number of children under six years and likely sources of lead, such as lead-based industries, homes built before 1940 (lead paint and pipes), and roads with high traffic volume.

Industrial sites using lead

Houses built before 1940

Roads with high traffic volume

High-risk areas

Lead exposure in Newark, New Jersey

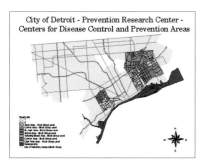

City of Detroit - Prevention Research Center - Centers for Disease Control and Prevention Areas

Raymond's students are working on a study comparing infant health in two Detroit neighborhoods.

"Babies born in the Latino community typically have higher birth weight and are healthier," Raymond notes. The researchers at the university are looking at cultural factors, like the kind of support young mothers get from their families, while Raymond's students focus on the physical conditions in the neighborhoods. For each block, the students come up with a score for each of ten factors, including the condition of the houses, the presence of garbage on the street, and others. "That enables us to do very thorough thematic maps," explains Raymond. The students will map the scores along with infant weight, immunization records, and other information, to see which factors might have the biggest impact on infant health. Public health agencies and community groups can then know better which conditions to relieve first.

Raymond's students have also used GIS to look into other vital issues facing the city.

In June of 1994, they worked with the Mayor's Office on a proposal to the federal government to create an urban empowerment zone in central Detroit. The program provides tax breaks and other incentives to stimulate business investment. "We actually moved our computer system into the Planning Department for ten days and worked there after school and over the weekend," recalls Raymond. He and his students used demographic information to help establish the boundary of the proposed empowerment zone. They also created maps, tables, and graphs to accompany the written proposal. "We were able to help with this project because we had the most up-to-date demographics with map-based referencing," says Raymond. The proposal resulted in a $100-million federal grant to create the empowerment zone.

Since 1993, when Raymond began using GIS in the classroom, almost 250 high school

Measuring water pollution in Dallas, Texas

Seventh- and eighth-graders at St. Monica's School in Dallas, Texas, used GIS to analyze pollution at White Rock Lake, a local recreation area. The students collected water samples and analyzed them for sediment, oil and other runoff, and pH. They then used GIS to map the locations of the samples, documenting the extent of the pollution. Finally, they presented their results to the city council. "We're pleased that a bond issue has been passed to dredge the lake. We feel we had something to do with that," says Principal Kate Collins.

"By the time kids get to be 11th and 12th graders, they are ready to go out and make a difference in their community. GIS provides that opportunity."

RANDY RAYMOND, TEACHER

students at Cass Tech and other area schools have been involved with GIS projects through the Urban Environmental Education in Detroit program. In the process of doing these projects, the students have gained valuable experience in using GIS and exploring the complex issues confronting the city. Many have turned that experience into paid internships at city agencies and local consulting firms. Some have chosen careers on the strength of it. Jenkins, for one, will soon enter a program at the University of Michigan leading to joint doctorate degrees in medicine and public health administration.

Raymond is gratified at how GIS is benefiting his students. "We can actually prepare them to look for ways of using information, and to identify problems that they can investigate and solve," he says. It's not just the students who benefit. "By the time kids get to be 11th and 12th graders, they are ready to go out and make a difference in their community," he adds. "GIS provides that opportunity."

The students created a series of maps that helped the City of Detroit win a $100-million grant from the federal government to establish an urban empowerment zone.

Police officers in Pittsburgh use GIS to track

trends in drug dealing and other crime.

11 Crime

In the predawn of a September morning, a hundred and fifty officers huddle in a cramped room at the Pittsburgh Police Department's downtown headquarters. The room is hushed as commanders brief the assembled narcotics officers and uniformed police. Meanwhile, the corner of Rosedale and Tioga streets in the Homewood South neighborhood, 4 miles east, is also quiet. By 4:00 A.M., the drug dealers who congregate here daily have all headed home.

Back at police headquarters, the briefing room begins to buzz with activity as the officers split into teams. Twenty minutes later a fleet of police cruisers silently converges on Rosedale and Tioga. At a few minutes past five, shouts and sirens jolt the neighborhood awake. TV camera crews record the action as officers bang on doors and roust the sleeping dealers. The arrests continue throughout the day—in Homewood South and across the city. Later that night, on the local TV news, the citizens of Pittsburgh watch the replay of the crackdown. The police hope both the dealers and the buyers will get the message that Homewood South is no longer a good place to do business.

Drug dealing and drug-related crime continues to be a big problem in many communities across the country. Drug activity can devastate a neighborhood as dealers take over the streets, assaults and shootings increase, and businesses move out, taking jobs with them. Many communities have chosen to confront the problem from all sides, including citizen block patrols, education, and job training. Law enforcement also plays a key role in helping the residents of these communities reclaim their neighborhoods.

"In the case of Homewood South, we had an open-air drug market that was right in the business area, and right where there were a lot of residents," says Commander Bill Bochter,

Pittsburgh, like any major city, has its share of crime. Police are working with community groups to help bring stability to the affected neighborhoods.

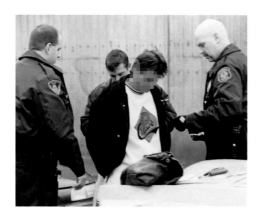

head of the Pittsburgh Police Department's Criminal Intelligence and Crime Analysis divisions. The corner of Rosedale and Tioga streets is what Bochter refers to as a historical drug marketplace. "Anybody knew you could go to Homewood South and get heroin or cocaine at this particular intersection," he explains. In early 1991 police began planning a drug sweep to disrupt the marketplace and bring some security to the neighborhood.

In June of that year they launched a three-month undercover sting operation. "Once we thought we had everybody who was dealing in that area, at least a buy or two on them, we decided it was time to have a roundup," recalls Bochter. In September, police staged the massive one-day operation to track down and arrest known drug dealers and buyers. Following the roundup, high-visibility narcotics

squads and uniformed officers began saturation patrols in and around the main area of drug activity at Rosedale and Tioga streets. "So the word gets out that this is a hot area," explains Bochter.

Bochter is realistic—he knows the drug activity won't disappear because of the sweep. "It's going to be displaced somewhere, and we try to manage that displacement," he says. To help monitor the movement of drug activity after a sweep, Bochter and the other officers in the Crime Analysis Division use a GIS-based program called DMAP. Andreas Olligschlaeger, a consultant working for the Pittsburgh Police Department, developed the Drug Market Analysis Program in 1990 using a grant from the U.S. Department of Justice.

The program maps the number of calls from each address where a resident has reported drug dealing or drug-related activity

As part of their efforts, police conduct drug sweeps to arrest both dealers and buyers, and disrupt known drug markets.

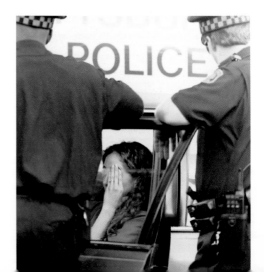

"DMAP helps us see where the new calls for service concerning drugs, guns, assaults, are starting to spring up."

BILL BOCHTER, COMMANDER

to the police. "DMAP helps us see where the new calls for service concerning drugs, guns, assaults, are starting to spring up," Bochter explains.

Following the drug sweep in Homewood South, Bochter asked Olligschlaeger to create a map showing the drug-related calls to 911 for the six months before and the six months after the sweep. Olligschlaeger entered the date of the sweep into DMAP along with the two dates six months on either side of it. The system searched all the calls to 911 during that period and selected the drug-related ones. It then drew the location of each call on a street map of Homewood South using a blue circle for calls that occurred before the drug roundup and a red circle for ones that occurred after. DMAP also drew the circles larger or smaller to show the number of calls from each address.

From the map, Bochter could clearly see the effect of the sweep. While there was still some drug activity at the intersection of Rosedale and Tioga, it had decreased significantly.

Some of the activity dispersed into the northwest section of the neighborhood. "We started to see a lot of back-alley drug distribution," Bochter explains. That meant the drug sweep had made it more difficult for the dealers to operate. "People from the suburbs knew they could come to that main street, buy their

Bochter used DMAP to see how drug dealing and other drug-related activity was displaced following a sweep. The blue dots show drug activity before the sweep, and the red dots, after.

drugs, and slip right back out of town." But once the market at Rosedale and Tioga disappeared, so did the suburban customers. "They didn't know the area well enough to start cruising alleys," says Bochter. Because the sweep disrupted the main drug market in the neighborhood, Bochter considers the action a success. "The people in this neighborhood finally got a break," he concludes.

Bochter and his officers now use DMAP to periodically look at drug activity in Homewood South to see if they need to go back in again. "DMAP helps us evaluate our efforts," he notes. "Did we react to where the new hot spots were flaring up? And when we

did, where did that displace to—did we properly manage it? In the case of Homewood South," he says, "it really hasn't come back to the degree it was five years ago."

Before the department had DMAP, officers stuck pins into a wall map to show the location of drug dealing. But that didn't show the intensity of the activity or the trends over time. Officers had to try to glean that information from reports. Explains Bochter, "They had to [read] that stack of reports and try to visualize those crimes in the area. It's very difficult." DMAP has changed all that. Says Olligschlaeger, "You give it to them on a map and it's right there. One look says it all."

Police also use DMAP to map drug activity in a neighborhood by time of day. Officers start by specifying a time period they want to look at, usually several months. DMAP draws a small pie chart at the location of each address where someone called 911 to report drug activity. The colors on the pie chart indicate the percentage of calls in each of four time slots: morning (red), afternoon (green), evening

Tracking gangs in Salinas, California

The City of Salinas Police Department is using GIS to help track guns and gang activity. Officers map the boundaries of known gang territories and can easily redraw the boundaries as they shift. They also map the locations of robberies, shootings, and other crimes involving handguns. The GIS helps them get advance warning of trouble, for instance when assaults start occurring more frequently at the border between two gang territories.

You can use GIS to map how a place has changed over time. That can help you assess the effect of past policies and actions. Police in Pittsburgh use GIS to track the change in drug-related activity in a neighborhood after a drug sweep.

What the system does...

1 *Queries the database.* The system selects all drug-activity calls from the E-911 database occurring six months before and six months after the drug sweep.

2 *Calculates the total occurrences.* For each time period, the system sums the number of calls made from each address.

3 *Draws the map.* The GIS uses the address to map the locations of the calls. It draws calls made before the sweep in blue, and calls made after, in red. It uses the size of the circles to indicate the number of calls from each

	1
	2 – 3
	4 – 7
	8 – 15

address. Police can see where activity decreased and where it moved to.

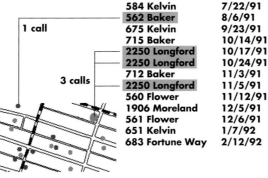

1887 Moreland	5/14/91
642 Kelvin	5/23/91
663 Kelvin	6/14/91
579 Fortune Way	7/11/91
1993 Moreland	7/18/91
584 Kelvin	7/22/91
562 Baker	8/6/91
675 Kelvin	9/23/91
715 Baker	10/14/91
2250 Longford	10/17/91
2250 Longford	10/24/91
712 Baker	11/3/91
2250 Longford	11/5/91
560 Flower	11/12/91
1906 Moreland	12/5/91
561 Flower	12/6/91
651 Kelvin	1/7/92
683 Fortune Way	2/12/92

More examples of using GIS to look at trends...

◆ The City of Adelaide, South Australia, used GIS to map the past expansion of the city. The Office of Housing and Urban Development mapped the age of houses and apartments to show which areas developed earlier, and which more recently. The maps are used by real estate agents and planners to track the overall growth of the city and surrounding areas.

◆ The City of Bellevue, Washington, used GIS to measure the change in summer water usage between 1991 and 1992. The city calculated the increase or decrease in water usage for each customer, and displayed the information on a map. The map was used to evaluate whether voluntary water restrictions were more effective in residential or commercial areas.

Other ways of looking at trends...

You can also look at trends by mapping how an activity changes within areas such as census tracts or police reporting districts. One way to do this is to create maps covering different time periods and compare them. Or you could have the GIS reveal trends by calculating how much the activity increased or decreased for each area.

Change in auto thefts in the City of Pittsburgh, 1994 to 1995, by census tract. Thefts decreased the most in tracts colored dark blue and increased in the bright red ones.

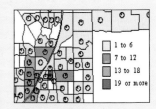
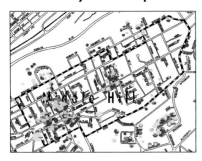

DMAP can create maps of drug activity by time of day. Drug-related activity reported during the daytime is shown in red and green; nighttime activity is shown in blue and yellow. The maps help police track the movement of drug dealers within a neighborhood over a twenty-four-hour period.

(blue), and late night (yellow). The size of the pie chart indicates how many total calls were made from that address. Says Olligschlaeger, "You can see some interesting patterns of how drug dealers move during the day in a five- or six-block area." For example, dealers may congregate near a school in the afternoon and move toward a business district in the evening. The information helps the commanders decide where to send officers, and when.

While the system began as a way of tracking drug activity, Bochter and the other officers now use it to look for patterns and trends in all types of crime. For instance, they create maps showing the locations of all auto thefts in the city over the course of a year. The areas that have a high number of thefts are immediately apparent. They've also used DMAP to create maps showing the increase or decrease

in number of auto thefts for each census tract in the city from year to year. That way police can keep tabs on long-term trends.

The department currently has three computers that run DMAP. Officers can get the information themselves, when they need it, rather than waiting for summary reports. "What we tried to do with DMAP was create a system that anybody can use with a half hour of training. We came pretty close to that goal," says Olligschlaeger.

DMAP creates maps using either 911 calls for service or actual arrests. The 911 data comes from the city's 911 Emergency Operations Center computer system. Arrest data comes from Pittsburgh's Public Safety Management System, a computer database maintained by the police department. The 911 system data is loaded into DMAP every two weeks and the arrest data is loaded weekly. Since DMAP uses information directly from these databases, the maps the officers create are always current.

Other map information used in DMAP, such as streets, building footprints, and parks, comes from the Pittsburgh Allegheny Geographic Information System (PAGIS), a GIS database developed by the city's planning department. DMAP also includes parcel information from the city's property tax files.

Olligschlaeger is planning to install DMAP on several more computers in the department so more officers can be trained on the system and use it on a day-to-day basis. His current work involves combining GIS with mathematical models to predict and map where drug activity will be high or low on a month-by-month basis. That way police can get a jump on the dealers.

With limited staff and money, the department needs the best information available to be most effective. "The police need analytical tools. They need graphical display of criminal activity and crime patterns," says Olligschlaeger. GIS is one tool that can provide such critical information. "It's probably one of the most innovative advances to hit information science in the last 10 to 15 years," states Olligschlaeger. Commander Bochter agrees: "It's been a hell of a tool for us."

The police use DMAP to track all types of crime, including auto theft. The size of each red circle indicates the number of reported thefts from that location. The information helps commanders decide where to assign additional officers.

Siting addiction prevention and treatment programs in Erie County, New York

Researchers at the New York State Research Institute on Addictions used GIS to help find the best locations for alcohol and drug programs in Erie County. They classified each census tract according to its need for addiction prevention and treatment—high, medium, or low—based on demographics, DWI convictions, and locations of bars and liquor stores. The study helped the county decide where to spend the limited funding available for addiction services.

Planners and neighborhood groups in Washoe County,

Nevada, use GIS to help plan the growth of the county

twenty years into the future.

12 Managing Growth

"The old-time residents are up in arms. They don't want a grocery store out here." Spanish Springs resident Jim Barrere is talking about a recent article in the *Reno Gazette-Journal.* A local supermarket chain has announced plans to build a new store at the corner of Pyramid Lake Highway and Spanish Springs Road, the main intersection in Spanish Springs. Right now, only the little Spanish Springs Market occupies the corner. Some long-time residents are concerned. They moved into this mostly undeveloped valley, a few miles north of Reno, Nevada, to be in the country. To them, the new supermarket is just the first step in losing that rural feel. They envision the worst: the intersection a maze of office parks and malls, Pyramid Lake Highway four lanes of bumper-to-bumper traffic, and the valley a sea of rooftops.

But that nightmare vision will never happen, according to Cynthia Albright, a growth management planner for Washoe County. Albright works with local residents to make sure Spanish Springs grows in a way that provides housing and public services for the future while maintaining the area's rural character.

There's no doubt that Spanish Springs is growing fast. In 1990 only 3,500 people lived in the valley. Projections by the Washoe County Department of Community Development show that by 2015 over 23,000 people will live there. New industry is bringing people into the area. Reno's hotels, casinos, nightclubs, and restaurants have also attracted a lot of people seeking work—over 40 percent of the jobs in Washoe County are in the service sector, primarily in tourism and retail. These jobs generally pay low salaries, but workers moving into the area still need housing. Developers have met that need by building less expensive houses in outlying areas, such as Spanish

Reno's growing economy is spurring the need for new housing, roads, libraries, and other services in the surrounding area.

Developers are building homes in outlying areas such as Spanish Springs Valley where land costs are lower than in the city.

Springs Valley, where land costs are lower than in the city. Out there, says Albright, developers can sell a single-family, three-bedroom, two-and-a-half-bathroom home with a third-acre of land for $129,000. In the city of Reno, just 12 miles down the road, the same house would cost about $200,000.

While developers are concerned with the immediate demand for housing, growth management planners at the county are concerned about the demand over the next twenty years. As John Hester, director of comprehensive planning for Washoe County, explains, "If the population is supposed to grow to 20,000, we make sure we have enough housing to handle 20,000 people."

But providing housing is only the beginning. With housing comes the need for stores, parks, schools, libraries, and fire stations. And more and wider roads to handle the increased traffic.

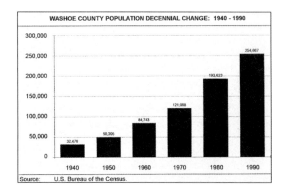

WASHOE COUNTY POPULATION DECENNIAL CHANGE: 1940 - 1990

Year	Population
1940	32,476
1950	50,205
1960	84,743
1970	121,068
1980	193,623
1990	254,667

Source: U.S. Bureau of the Census.

The danger, as Barrere puts it, is "growth that wants to come in pockets—a pocket of houses here, a pocket there." That eventually leads to widespread development. "When you start filling in between those pockets you start creating gridlock and congestion," continues Barrere.

To prevent that, Albright worked with Barrere and other members of the Spanish Springs Citizen Advisory Board (CAB) to create a twenty-year plan for Spanish Springs. The plan covers everything from maintaining air quality to projecting how many new schools will be needed. Underlying it all is a map that shows which parts of the valley will be developed, and which won't. Albright used GIS to help create the map.

Albright's goal was to make sure there was enough land designated for housing and other services to meet the needs of the 23,000 people projected to live in the area in 2015. At the same time, she had a mandate from current residents to maintain the rural character of the valley.

Albright first used the GIS to map all the land in the area that is off limits for development. Some land is unsuitable because it's either too steep, in a floodplain or a wetland, or is publicly owned. The "development suitability" map shows all the areas that fall into one of these categories, using a different color for each. The remaining land on the map is suitable for development.

Of course, some of that land has already been developed. There are about 230 homes on 5- and 10-acre lots scattered around the valley. Several newer subdivisions with smaller lots have also been built, providing housing for about 4,000 people. The location of this existing development was also mapped using the GIS.

The maps of suitable land and existing development were printed from the GIS and used

"Using GIS, we significantly reduce the level of error. If you find a mistake, you can correct it easily. It's a tremendous time saver."

CYNTHIA ALBRIGHT, PLANNER

in a series of public meetings. By comparing the maps, planners and residents of the area could see where housing, stores, and other

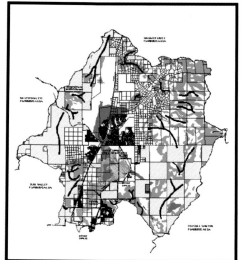

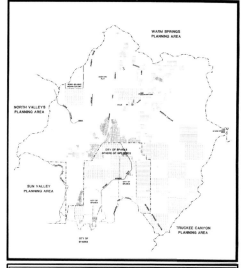

Planners and residents use maps showing existing land use and areas suitable for development, along with population forecasts, to help decide where new housing should be built.

development would be appropriate. It had to be on suitable land. And ideally, it would be near existing development to reduce the need for new roads, sewers, and other public facilities. That would also leave large tracts of land around the edges of the valley undeveloped. Once the planners and residents identified areas appropriate for the various land uses, they drew the boundaries on a paper map. This map was also digitized and put into the GIS.

Copies of the map were given to each of the county agencies responsible for building the roads, sewers, parks, libraries, schools, and other public facilities that future residents of the area will need. Each agency used the map to help figure out where new facilities would go, and when they should be built. Albright put the locations of these facilities into the GIS and created a map showing them along with existing facilities.

The map of planned land use is used to help guide development and show where, and when, new roads, schools, parks, and other facilities will need to be built.

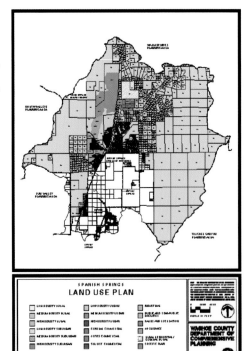

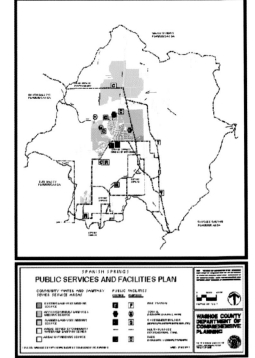

You can use GIS to help plan what a place will be like in the future. That gives a community the time it needs to provide housing, facilities, and other services. Planners at Washoe County, Nevada, use GIS to help create twenty-year plans for areas within the county.

What they do...

1 Forecast future growth. Based on how population has grown in the past, planners predict how it will grow in each area over the next twenty years.

2 Map what's already there. They use GIS to create maps showing where the existing population lives, what the land use is, where roads are, and so on. They also map which undeveloped areas are suitable for future growth.

3 Develop the plan. Using the GIS-generated maps, planners work with community groups to make sure enough land is set aside for the housing and other services needed to support the projected population growth over the next twenty years. They use GIS to create maps showing where the new housing and other services should be built, and to calculate how much land is allocated to the different types of housing.

4 Put the plan into practice. The various agencies that provide the services (police, schools, libraries, and so on) use GIS to create maps of each phase of the plan as it develops—for example, which parks are built and which are still planned, and where water and sewer lines have been put in.

5 Make revisions. As population forecasts and the needs of the community change, the community groups and the planners use GIS to make changes to the plan and create revised maps and figures.

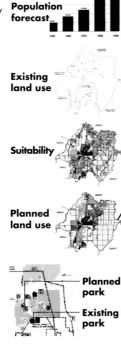

Population forecast

Existing land use

Suitability

Planned land use

Planned park

Existing park

How GIS helps make the plan...

◆ Information from a variety of maps and databases can be combined in the GIS and displayed on one map or on a series of them.

◆ The GIS lets you combine data to create new information about a place. For example, you could combine digital maps of soils, slopes, and land cover to find areas suitable for building on (e.g., areas having suitable soils, on a gradual slope, and not on a wetland).

◆ Since all edits are made on the computer, it's easy to map several different scenarios or make changes to the maps. When you're ready, you can print as many copies of the maps as you need, right from the GIS.

More examples of using GIS to plan for the future...

◆ The William S. Hart Union High School District in Santa Clarita, California, uses GIS to help forecast student enrollment seven years into the future. They collect and analyze demographic and development data for each neighborhood. That tells them where and when they will need to build new schools.

◆ A private consulting firm used GIS to help develop a master plan for the City of Kuwait by integrating information on population, construction, and employment. The plan will help the city tackle long-term development issues, as well as provide a guide for day-to-day decisions such as evaluating building permits.

Managing capital improvements in Albuquerque, New Mexico

Planners at the City of Albuquerque use GIS to track the status of such projects as street and storm drain improvements, parks, and libraries. They create maps by council district showing which projects are planned, which in design, and which under construction. The GIS is also used to help coordinate budgets and schedules between city departments.

All the maps were included in the twenty-year plan for Spanish Springs. County officials use the plan to ensure that Spanish Springs will grow in a way that meets the needs of the community.

Albright now uses the GIS to keep track of how Spanish Springs grows. She calculates the total number of building permits for different types of housing approved by the county each year (single-family, condominium, and so forth). That number is then entered into a spreadsheet. Using 2.5 people per household as an average, she calculates the number of new residents moving into the area every year. A computer model uses past and current growth to forecast the population for the next twenty years. Albright then uses the GIS to calculate how much land has been set aside for each type of housing. That way she can make sure there will be enough housing—of different types—to meet the needs of the future population. She can also link her computer directly to the county tax assessor's GIS database to create maps. That lets her get a current

picture of the existing land use in the valley, as the lots are developed.

And as the county funds specific capital improvement projects, Albright uses the GIS to find parcels of land the right size that are already in public ownership or in default for unpaid taxes. The county can then look at acquiring these parcels for the public projects.

Before they had the GIS, Albright and other planners at the county created all the maps by hand. When population projections required changes to the land use boundaries, planners would have to erase and redraw the lines on paper maps. To find out how much land was allotted to the various uses, the planners would measure each area using a planimeter or scale. And creating copies of the maps for public hearings, for the CAB, or for other agencies was expensive—the maps had to be sent out to be photographically reproduced.

Now planners can easily change land use areas right on the computer screen. The GIS does any calculations automatically. Says Albright, "Using GIS, we significantly reduce the level of error. If you find a mistake you can correct it easily. It's a tremendous time saver." When the maps are final, planners can print as many copies as needed, right in the planning department office. "We can print out twenty-five maps in a half hour at a tenth of the cost to draw one and send it out for color reprographics," explains Albright.

The GIS uses information from various sources. Planners in the Growth Management section of the department, along with a consulting firm hired by the county, created the map of suitable land. They combined information from aerial photos, U.S. Soil Conservation Service soil type maps, state geological maps, and data from the county tax assessor. Some of the data was already in digital format. Planning department staff digitized the rest from paper maps. The map of existing land use is based on the county tax assessor's parcel database. Each parcel is tagged with a code that indicates its current land use. This information is also stored in the GIS.

Spanish Springs is just one of twelve planning areas within Washoe County. Albright and the other growth management planners have created a twenty-year plan for each. And although each area is unique, GIS has played a similar role in each one.

In Spanish Springs, GIS helps Albright plan a future that accommodates growth while maintaining the rural character of the area. Says CAB member Barrere, "It's kind of a compromise for everybody." The county revises the plan every five years, so the next plan will consider what Spanish Springs might be like in 2020. There are certain to be new and different issues. As Barrere concludes, "The personality of the valley changes as it grows." And GIS helps make it easier to plan for that growth.

Planning future transportation for San Diego, California

The San Diego Association of Governments uses GIS to plan routes for public transportation. Planners used forecasts of population and employment for 2015 to develop a map showing how many people per day, on average, will be using express and local bus routes, commuter rail, and the San Diego Trolley. The map helps planners see where they'll need to make new routes, and which routes may need buses and trains to run more frequently.

Afterword

Over the past few decades, GIS technology spread slowly, often by word of mouth. In many communities, GIS was first used by one person for one specific task. Now, GIS is widespread throughout these communities, used by local governments, utility companies, and private businesses alike.

A dramatic increase in the amount and quality of geographic data has helped enable the spread of GIS. Over the years, people collected data about their communities and assembled it into GIS databases. Local organizations are now finding that by sharing this data, they can coordinate with each other better and be more efficient.

Today, the use of GIS is poised to reach even greater levels as the technology becomes accessible to more people in many new ways. Towns and cities are putting GIS in libraries and other public locations, so people can get information about their communities. Both local governments and private companies are using GIS to make maps and other geographic information available over the World Wide Web. Neighborhood groups and small businesses are discovering that they can use GIS on their desktop and laptop computers.

There are now many ways to use GIS, and many places to find out about it. The Internet is a good place to start. If you have access to the World Wide Web, you can just search for "GIS." You'll turn up lots of sites that are using GIS, as well as sources of software and data.

Several magazines are dedicated to GIS and related technologies. *GIS World* (970-223-4848 or www.geoplace.com) and *Geo Info Systems* (800-346-0085 or www.geoinfosystems.com) cover the full range of GIS applications. *Business Geographics* (published by *GIS World*) is geared toward retail and other business uses of GIS.

Many books about GIS are available, covering a wide range of topics. Some can be found in the computer section of your local bookstore, or in technical or college bookstores. Many can be ordered through the magazines mentioned above. ESRI (800-447-9778 or www.esri.com), the publisher of this book, also publishes a catalog of books on GIS and mapping.

As you explore these sources, you'll see that GIS has many uses beyond the local community. GIS is being used by state and federal agencies to manage water, forests, and wildlife. It's used by universities to track social trends across the country. It's used by private companies to develop national marketing strategies, and to move goods and information around the planet. GIS has even been used to map Mars.

At the community level, though, GIS is having a direct impact on people's daily lives. Whatever your needs and interests, and however you go about it, hopefully you will explore GIS and think about how you can use it where you work and live. But even if you never use GIS, you now know how digital maps are making life better in communities everywhere, probably even yours.

Photo and Map Credits

Photos

All photographs by ESRI, except as noted below.

p. 6	Kennebunk Communications Center, Kennebunk, Maine
p. 18	Sears Logistics Service, Inc., Hoffman Estates, Illinois
p. 20	Sears Logistics Service, Inc., Hoffman Estates, Illinois
p. 38	City of Greenville, South Carolina
p. 40	City of Greenville, South Carolina
p. 42	City of Greenville, South Carolina
p. 66	Metro–Regional Environmental Management Department, Portland, Oregon
p. 71	Metro–Regional Environmental Management Department, Portland, Oregon
p. 74	Star Enterprise, Houston, Texas
p. 75	Star Enterprise, Houston, Texas
p. 76	Star Enterprise, Houston, Texas
p. 77	Star Enterprise, Houston, Texas
p. 78	Star Enterprise, Houston, Texas
p. 80	Star Enterprise, Houston, Texas
p. 83	Cass Technical High School, Detroit, Michigan
p. 84	Cass Technical High School, Detroit, Michigan
p. 89	Cass Technical High School, Detroit, Michigan
p. 90	Marc Fader, Pittsburgh, Pennsylvania
p. 91	Joel B. Levinson–Pittsburghscape, Pittsburgh, Pennsylvania
p. 92	Marc Fader, Pittsburgh, Pennsylvania
p. 93	Pittsburgh Bureau of Police, Pittsburgh, Pennsylvania

Maps

pp. 4–5	Town of Kennebunk, Maine
p. 8	Tacoma Fire Department, City of Tacoma, Washington
pp. 12–13	Philadelphia Association of Community Development Corporations, Philadelphia, Pennsylvania
p. 17	City of Louisville Department of Public Works, Louisville, Kentucky
pp. 21–22	Sears Merchandise Group, Hoffman Estates, Illinois, and ESRI, Redlands, California
p. 25	Davis Demographics and Planning, Corona, California
p. 26	Sears Merchandise Group, Hoffman Estates, Illinois, and ESRI, Redlands, California
p. 27	Radio Satellite Integrators, Inc., Torrance, California
pp. 30–31	Bexar Appraisal District, San Antonio, Texas

CONTINUED

Maps (continued)

Index